Play Golf the Wright Way

PLAY GOLF
THE
WRIGHT WAY

Dec '21

Linda

MICKEY WRIGHT

Edited by Joan Flynn Dreyspool

Foreword by Tom Watson

*Hey Linda hope this
wonderful game brings as much
Joy to your life as it has
to mine*

*Always
Glenn*

Taylor Publishing Company
Dallas, Texas

Published by Taylor Publishing Company
        1550 West Mockingbird Lane
        Dallas, Texas 75235

This is an authorized reprint of the original edition
published by Doubleday in 1962.

Library of Congress Cataloging-in-Publication Data

Wright, Mickey, 1935-
    Play golf the Wright way / Mickey Wright ; photographs by Robert Riger.
        p.   cm.
    Originally published: Garden City, N.Y. : Doubleday, 1962.
    ISBN 0-87833-812-8
    ISBN 0-87833-813-6 (pbk.)
    1. Swing (Golf)   I. Title.
  GV979.S9W75   1993
  796.352'3—dc20   92-37340
                                             CIP

Printed in the United States of America

10 9 8 7 6 5 4 3 2 1

CONTENTS

FOREWORD
TO THE NEW EDITION
by Tom Watson

WHEN I was a boy, my father's great passion for golf quickly won my full attention. He was a vital, early influence in my golfing life. Mickey Wright's experience was the same. In this new edition of her entertaining and informative classic, she tells the story of getting a set of toy clubs from her dad at the age of four, clubs she immediately destroyed by swinging them as hard as she could. But with patience and encouragement her father got her started.

Fathers are often key figures and the first teachers for young golfers. I remember those early days on the course, at the practice tee and on the putting green. Dad would be watching, correcting mistakes, encouraging me. But the best memories are the conversations and arguments Dad and his buddies would have over two topics: who was the greatest golfer of all time, and who had the greatest swing.

Dad's passion for Sam Snead's rhythm always dominated any conversation centered around the phrase "the greatest." Dad's love of the game, his passion for golf, has been exceeded by few others I have known. I loved his talk about—and admiration for—the great players of the game. He thought Byron Nelson had achieved the greatest winning streak and that it would never, ever be broken. Dad said so, and Dad knew, and that's all there was to it for this kid.

And my father's expert eyes saw something very special in the golf swing of Mickey Wright. He had watched her in Pointe Clear, Alabama, at the Lakewood Country Club, and he had seen her on television. He said she had the most beautiful golf swing of any woman he had ever seen. Because of Dad's instrumental influence on me, because I had watched and read anything concerning golf at that tender age, and because I was crazy about all sports, I became an instant Mickey Wright fan. After all, anyone with the same name as my heroes—Mantle and Mouse—had to be someone super special.

I began to watch for Mickey Wright on television and I read everything I could about her career. That was easy, for she was in the news every week as she dominated the LPGA tour with that beautiful swing. She won thirteen victories in just one year! She did it with her entire golf game, of course, but it was built around that swing. In these days it is politically incorrect to say so, but she swung a golf club just like a man, with great rhythm and power. There was no looseness; it was simple movement, yet the acceleration was what I had always reserved for the male golf swing. That grace and strength from a lovely woman… it was clear that power and distance were now significant factors in a woman's golf game.

Many of us felt that Mickey retired from the game too early—right at her peak, it seems in retrospect. It was such a joy to see her hit a golf ball: an amazing display of beautiful rhythm, unwasted power, perfect balance. Dad was unmistakably correct. This is one of the greatest swings in golf, man or woman.

Mickey doesn't tee it up on television these days. But after thirty years we now have the complete story of the great lady's great swing back in print in this new edition.

Welcome back, Mickey.

INTRODUCTION
TO THE NEW EDITION

"A SWING is a Swing is a Swing," I wrote when *Play Golf the Wright Way* was first published.

Since then, the Game of Golf and its accessories have undergone some radical changes. Luckily for us all, the basic fundamentals of the golf swing are constant. My thoughts and teachings on balance, footwork, timing, rhythm, square clubface, good grip, practice habits, and emotional control have not changed over the decades.

"Golf is the only sport where the ball doesn't move until you hit it," Baseball Hall of Famer Ted Williams once told me. Think about it! You've got all the finest modern hi-tech equipment available: faster balls, sleeker shafts, lighter weights, fancy irons, gloves that fit, shoes built for support, specially designed clothes to ease the freedom of your swing. Yardages are calculated. Your target is in your mind. You've selected your club. Everything's set for the shot.

The ball is there waiting for you to hit it. Where it goes is up to you, hi-tech notwithstanding.

Back to the basics. Stance. Grip. Balance. Rhythm. Clubface square at address and throughout the swing. You are in complete control. If you build a repetitive, self-sustaining swing, it will sustain you now and through all your golfing years to come, and I hope they are many.

Golf has been good to me, and I have always given my best to Golf. Though I retired fairly early from competition on a regular basis, in 1969, because I could no longer give the Tour full-time commitment, my devotion to the game and joy in swinging a golf club have never diminished.

Looking back, my only regret is that when I started golf at such a young age, I was so entranced with the magic of hitting the ball long I didn't practice enough on the short game. For beginning golfers reading this book, and for older ones, too, to lower your scores, I would stress the chapter on Stroke Savers and encourage you to spend a great part of your practice time around the greens.

I am honored to be a member of the LPGA's Hall of Fame. I am grateful for every win. I never hit a golf shot in my entire life that I didn't try to do my best.

If my love for, dedication to, and performance in the Game of Golf put me in the record books for now and maybe hereafter, I am indeed rewarded.

In recent years, I have had many inquiries from people wanting to know how they could get a copy of this book. I'm glad it's now back in print.

I'd like to dedicate it to all the golf teachers, past and present and future, who selflessly dedicate themselves to building better golfers.

MICKEY WRIGHT

Port St. Lucie, Florida
1993

Play Golf the Wright Way

THE WARM-UP

BEFORE a competitive round of golf, I warm-up by hitting from twenty to thirty balls. I don't look for anything special in my swing at this time. All I want is feel, feel of the weight of the clubhead and a conscious awareness of the position of the clubhead throughout my swing.

I am always in search of the positive approach to golf, so much so that I de-emphasize the negative. I am not going to give you any remedies for what will happen if you don't do what I tell you. That would be like a doctor's saying, "I'm going to give you these pills that should cure you, but in case you don't take these pills, then here are some other pills for the disease you're going to get if you don't take these pills that I prescribe in the first place."

I have this same affirmative approach to those prevalent ills of the game of golf, "Keep Your Head Down," "Worry About Your Hips," and "Think of Your Hands." The incidence of occurrence of these ailments is high among golfers, much too high, and again so unnecessary. They are purely clinical cases where the patient is suffering from a disease caused by not having taken the right medicine in the beginning.

I, therefore, am not going to treat anybody for any subsidiary symptoms resulting from not following my initial prescription. A sound efficient swing (with the basic ingredients of balance, rhythm, and a square clubhead position throughout) is a powerful antibiotic for the chronic complainer on the golf course. I'm particularly unsympathetic to the sick golfer who knows something is radically wrong with his game but will never go to the practice tee to correct it. I've written an entire chapter on "Practice Can Be Fun." This sugar-coating the pill for practice is a must, the fixative in my prescription for a bigger, better, and healthier game of golf. If you are not prepared to practice, consult another golf specialist.

As a professional golf practitioner, I have read many text books on the subject and I am convinced that the best way to learn from a book is by studying pictures of a good golf swing. It is easier to show a person how to swing a golf club than it is to tell him. For that reason there are lots of pictures of my swing in this book.

In my captions, I have tried to select the pivotal points in each picture

7

that will best give you a visual and descriptive understanding of the swing. I have tried sincerely to place a stethoscope upon the heart and arteries of my swing and thinking.

May I suggest that when you've read the text and studied the pictures that you conduct a "monkey see, monkey do" experiment. Select some of the swing positionings that especially appeal to you and imitate them. Assume the exact position I'm in and then try to feel what you think I feel when I am in those positions. This will alert your muscles to that positioning and help give you a mental picture which you can develop in the swing itself.

Because I know most people like to look at the pictures first and read the text afterward, I'm starting off with two photographic sequences right at the beginning of the book. Since the driver is the club I am most identified with, because of my distance, I'm starting off with the driver somewhat against my better judgment. Swing-wise, the best club to start with to create or improve a swing is the wedge, the heaviest club in the bag. Its weight enables you to feel the clubhead more, so for your own

The Driver: Side-View

Figure 1 Address position with driver; slightly closed stance, weight balanced from ball of feet back toward heels, right elbow slightly lower than left. Inside of left elbow visible from behind, knees slightly flexed.

Figure 2 First move away from ball; clubhead being swept back very low.

sake always start with the wedge. For this book, however, I'll begin with the driver.

I didn't mention it in the captions, but look at my jaw-clenching determination to hit that ball as hard as I possibly can. That's one of the secrets of hitting a long ball, give it all you've got.

That's what I've tried to give you.

When I was twelve years old, I was given a copy of Patty Berg's golf book. Every night when I went to bed, I'd study the illustrations of Patty's swing and try to imagine myself in the various positions.

How does she feel when she does that? I'd ask myself. Then I'd visualize myself swinging and feeling the same way. I didn't realize it at the time, but I was forming a "good study habit," for subconsciously I was conditioning my mind and my muscles to react to a given circumstance. This is the same training method used to indoctrinate the orbiting chimpanzees for their guided swings around the earth; conditioned reflexes under duress, which certainly is applicable to the stress and strain of a pressurized golf swing.

Figure 3 Weight transferring to right foot; club-head, hands, arms, shoulders, hips turning together as a one-piece move.

Figure 4 Halfway position in backswing; club-head square, arms and hands in relatively same position to body as at address, weight moving across left foot onto inside right foot.

Figure 5　At this point shoulders and hips have turned as much as they will on backswing and weight has shifted to inside right foot, right leg and right knee.

Figure 6　Momentum of clubhead is swinging arms and hands to completed and fully cocked position at top of swing.

Figure 9　Only difference here from figure 8 is weight is starting to move back to left foot and left heel is starting to settle back down to ground. Right elbow has just begun its move back into right side, otherwise no noticeable change in position of clubhead, hands, shoulders, or hips.

Figure 10　Especially notice right elbow now well tucked into right side. Hands and wrists are still in about same cocked position as at top of swing. Even though weight is noticeably driving toward left foot, my head is held behind ball.

Figure 7 Nearing the top of a smooth, well-co-ordinated swing.

Figure 8 Top of backswing; right elbow pointed toward ground, line from right armpit to elbow parallel to ground, clubhead square, 90 degree shoulder turn, 45 degree hip turn, weight on inside right foot, leg, knee, right knee still bent or flexed as at address position.

Figure 12 Immediately after impact; clubhead still square, right shoulder working under rather than around as result of right elbow being tucked in on entire downswing. Note kicking off or thrusting action of right foot.

Figure 11 Compare clubhead position here to figure 5. Clubhead position still square.

Figure 13 Continued releasing of right side through ball, eyes starting to follow flight of ball.

Figure 14 Right hand naturally crossed over. This is real important.

The Driver: Front-View

Figure 17 The one-piece move away from ball is approximately two to three feet underway here. Most outstanding point is arms and hands have stayed in same relationship to shoulders and body as at address (see figure 1). This is what I mean by staying relatively square throughout a golf swing.

Figure 18 Continuation of one-piece move with no apparent effort to do anything whatsoever with hands other than hold on to club and follow shifting of weight and body turn.

Figure 15 Finish of swing; compare to figure 8, top of backswing. Left elbow now pointed toward ground, right arm extended in reverse of left arm extension at top of backswing. Weight completely transferred to left foot. A belt buckle would be pointing directly toward your target.

Figure 16 Completely relaxed, well-balanced expenditure of finish. If you have been in balance throughout swing, you can stand and hold finish several seconds.

Figure 19 Halfway back; square position, left hand extended properly and comfortably in what I term "Shake hands" position.

Figure 20 Dramatically illustrates the stretching of muscles in back and left side as club nears top of swing.

Figure 21 This stretch has come about through resistance set up from gripping-in of right foot and inside muscles of right leg. *The recoiling from this stretch on the downswing is what gives me my power, clubhead speed and distance.*

Figure 22 Top of swing; shows well right hand under club in tray-carrying position, clubface square, weight well transferred to right foot, right leg and knee still flexed in its supporting yet ready-to-spring position.

Figure 25 This right elbow movement has helped me keep my hands in still cocked position, as they were at top of backswing, as long as possible, to ready them for the hit.

Figure 26 After impact; eyes still looking at spot where ball was.

Figure 23   First move of downswing; returning of weight toward left foot has started, left hip turning, hands have remained fully cocked and are merely going along for the ride at this point.

Figure 24   This and figure 25 *must be* helpful. Notice as weight continues to move to left side that right elbow has started its move down into right side in front of right hipbone.

Figure 27   Now almost a reverse negative of body halfway at backswing, shoulders turned 90 degrees, hips turned 45 degrees, right arm extended in handshake position, reversal of left arm position in figure 19, left elbow pointed toward ground, weight on left foot.

Figure 28   Transfer of weight to left completed, hands finished high, good balance maintained.

Figure 29 Finish of swing, completely relaxed
with eyes following flight of ball.

I am a golf professional and a perfectionist so I don't expect an amateur
to approach the game with the same dedication as I do, but every little
bit you do will help you and your golf swing. Don't just look at these
pictures and scan the captions and text and dismiss them from your mind
and muscle image. Do what I did when I was twelve.

Try to get the "feel" of my swing and thinking—or anyone else's for that
matter, whomsoever's swing you admire. What I want is for you to give
as much as you can of yourself to get the utmost out of your game of golf.

Chapter I

THIS ONE'S ON ME

WHEN I was seven years old, my father bought me a toy set of golf clubs from a dime store in San Diego, my home town. I swung so hard with those little tin clubs I broke every one of them.

I still swing hard. But now I know what I'm doing.

After my first disastrous venture into golf, I didn't swing a club again until I was eleven, a blond, chunky, oversized girl, 5'9", my present height. I'm grateful now that I'm tall for I have long arms which give me a long arc and help me to hit a longer ball, but when I was eleven and big for my age, I would have given anything to be small and dainty like Johna Lou Kimball who lived down the street.

If I had been small and dainty like Johna Lou, I've wondered since, would I have taken up golf with the zest and zeal that I did?

Something happened to me when I swung a golf club. I felt free and graceful and like somebody. I still do. Golf to me is not only a way of life, it's a creative outlet, a constant, never-ending challenge; frustrating, but never dull; infuriating, but satisfying.

Golf has brought me more rewards, financially and personally, than I ever could have earned had I become the psychology teacher I set out to be when I enrolled in Leland Stanford University at Palo Alto, California, in the summer session of 1952. I never finished college or the course, for in November 1954, when I was nineteen, I became a professional golfer and the youngest member on the tour of the Ladies Professional Golf Association. I feel as if I've earned my own version of a master's degree in psychology in study and experience, trial and error on golf courses throughout the United States, for psychology, I've learned, is as integral a part of good golf as an efficient swing.

I was born on Valentine's Day, 1935, and christened Mary Kathryn after my mother, Kathryn, a beautiful Southern belle from Atlanta, Georgia. My father, Arthur F. Wright, a successful San Diego attorney and one-time president of the California State Bar Association, was fifty-two when I was born. He wanted a boy and had the name Michael picked out. When Michael turned out to be Mary Kathryn, he compromised and nicknamed me "Mickey."

Figure 30

My parents were divorced when I was three. Each has remarried. My father, a former football player at the University of Michigan, enjoyed sports of all kinds. He thought I could be a good athlete more as a form of self-expression than as a career. I started to walk when I was nine months old and my co-ordination always has been good. Dad bought me a baseball glove and bat when I was four, and used to get out in his backyard and pitch to me and throw the ball so hard my hands would hurt from catching it.

Unwittingly, he was contributing to my becoming a good golfer, for "ball sense" is a great asset to a woman golfer. The instinctive feeling of normal release in throwing a ball, with the same underhand, natural reflex action as pitching a horseshoe or lagging a penny finds its counterpart in golf, especially in the short game and putting where judgment of distance is the main objective.

My father liked golf. An average player with the analytical mind of an attorney, he worked constantly at understanding and improving his game. Frequently, when he went to a driving range to practice, he took me along. So at the ripe age of eleven, I, too, had my cubicle on the practice tee, a bucket of balls, and a borrowed club. Hour after hour, I stood swinging away with all my might. All I wanted to do was hit, hit, hit, the more the merrier.

Finally, brimming over with enthusiasm and self-confidence, characteristics uncharacteristic of me at the age of eleven, I pestered my father to let me play golf with him at the La Jolla Country Club, about 18 miles from San Diego. This was more than he had bargained for so he did what any good lawyer would do. He asked for a postponement.

"Take some lessons first and *then* I'll play golf with you," he promised.

And so I met Johnny Bellante, the golf professional at the La Jolla Country Club (and now the pro at the Chapultepec Country Club in Mexico City). Johnny was about forty, handsome, dark-haired, a fine teacher and a beautiful swinger of the golf club. He had unlimited patience, besides, which he needed with me.

I'll never forget that first lesson. Like an overwhelming Newfoundland puppy, not quite housebroken but willing to make up in floppy affection what I lacked in behavior, I showed up on the practice tee, wearing sneakers and pedal pushers and an "I'll-show-you-how-far-I-can-hit-the-ball" expression.

Johnny had trained puppies before; a soothing voice, a kind word, but you must obey the master's commands. I obeyed. There is no better time to learn golf than when you are young and anxious and willing and uncomplicated. You don't question anything the teacher tells you. You just do it

19

like a little monkey. Your body is agile and limber. Your muscles respond. Your immature mind doesn't dominate the swing.

From the very beginning, Johnny tried to teach me the feeling of a free, rhythmic, gradually accelerating swing; to reach the maximum speed or momentum at contact, another secret of hitting the ball long.

Johnny made a switch from a eucalyptus tree branch, handed it to me and said, "Mickey, I want you to swing this until you can make it sing."

To make that switch sing, I had to move it as correctly as I would a golf club. I discovered that it reached its highest pitch at the bottom point of the swing. If I tried to make it sing by swinging it from on top, by forcibly assisting it with my body, my arms, my hands, my shoulders, it wouldn't sing. It wouldn't even groan. It just wasted its momentum and wound up limp, spent and ineffective.

To make that switch sing, I literally had to let it have its head to reach its own normal momentum and to delay the blow until the switch had returned to its original address position, then it would truly sing.

I took lessons from Johnny Bellante for three years. He was also Gene Littler's first teacher, and it must have given Johnny great satisfaction in 1961 when two of his protégés from the same town, Gene Littler and Mary Kathryn Wright, won the Men and Women's United States Opens. I know it did me. I had won it twice before, in 1958 and 1959, but each time I win the Open—and I hope I win it many more times—there is the secret satisfaction of a little girl with a most cherished possession.

Johnny also worked on balance and rhythm with me, two "musts" in any good golf swing. No matter how they swing, all good golfers have one thing in common, balance and rhythm.

To teach me balance, Johnny had me stand on one foot and swing, then he had me stand with my feet close together and swing.

If you can swing from either of these positions without toppling over, then you have an inkling of what a balanced swing should feel like.

By summer's end, I got so I could pretty regularly hit a ball 175 or 200 yards. Johnny was so pleased with his pupil he telephoned the San Diego *Union* and asked the newspaper to send out a photographer. The *Union* not only printed my picture but captioned it questioningly, "The Next Babe?"

What I liked best about the picture was the fact that my schoolmates at Woodrow Wilson Junior High saw it and looked at me, I thought, with a tinge of admiration and respect. That was my first taste of recognition. I savor it still.

There are times when I think I always had a good swing, but I have home movies of my first six months of learning which tell me differently and help to keep me humble. In them, I look like the worst woodchopper imaginable with a typical beginner's swing; a bad grip, a closed clubface going away from the ball and a flying right elbow which pointed away from the ground at the top of the swing. At the start of the downswing I worked the club to the outside and cut across the ball, a perfect slice or push position.

Figure 31   LEFT to RIGHT: Paul Runyan, the famous pro; Gene Littler and myself. Gene and I are both 1961 Open Champions. We are also both San Diegans who studied under Johnny Bellante, and in 1961 were voted San Diego's "Athletes of the Year."

Apart from my school work and activities, golf became my all-encompassing passion. Slowly I lost interest in Tommy Goodbody, my childhood beau and dancing partner. Every chance I had, I'd play golf or take a lesson or practice by myself. La Jolla Country Club is full of canyons and I managed to visit five or six of them in each round of golf. Inevitably I had three or four unplayable lies. I was long and I was wild and I loved every minute of it. It usually took me two or three shots to get out of a sand trap, I three-putted practically every green. Slowly but surely, things began to fall into place.

At the end of the first year, I broke 100, still one of my greatest golfing thrills. The second year I broke 90, and the fourth year, when I was fifteen, I shot a 70 at the Mission Valley Country Club in San Diego in a local city tournament. I remember playing with Millie Rebstock, the city and county champion at the time. That day everything went together.

After three years of working with Johnny Bellante, I studied a year with Fred Sherman, then pro at the Mission Valley Country Club, coincidentally now the site of the Mickey Wright Open, a new annual event on the LPGA tour.

An ardent pupil, I put my teachers on a pedestal, and tried my best to do anything they told me to do. I practiced faithfully, out of desire, not coercion.

In 1949, I played in the Southern California Junior Girls Tournament at the San Gabriel Country Club. I won it and won as well the discerning professional interest of Harry Pressler, the club pro.

"If you ever feel you need further help in your golf swing, I'll be happy to help you," he told me.

Before too long, with my mother's permission, I telephoned Mr. Pressler. "This is Mickey Wright. Do you remember me? I can use your help."

"Are you going to be home tonight?" he asked. That very evening Harry Pressler drove all the way from Los Angeles to San Diego, had dinner with us and spent four hours giving me a lesson in the living room.

We had a big mirror there, and Harry worked on my position at the top of the swing. In that and the many lessons that followed, for which he never charged me, Harry indoctrinated me with the principle of keeping the clubface square throughout the swing; at address position; halfway through the backswing; at the top of the swing; at impact and halfway through the finish of the swing.

This is the theory I subscribe to today. To achieve and maintain this square position throughout, Harry also emphasized the need and logic of rolling the weight across my feet from the left foot to the inside of the right. That was then and still is foreign to many golfers, but to me it is the mainspring of my swing.

A day or so after my living-room lesson with Harry Pressler, I played in the Indio (California) Invitational Tournament and won it with rounds of 70 and 71. For two years thereafter, every Saturday morning my mother drove me the 125 miles to Los Angeles so I could take a lesson from Harry.

Hour after hour we worked on the key points of the swing. Harry actually placed me in those "square" positions so I could learn the feel.

I practiced it so thoroughly and painstakingly that to me now *a swing is a conscious feeling of the weight and position of the clubhead at all times throughout the swing.*

Yet with all the fine teaching I had as a young girl, it took me almost six years on the LPGA tour to learn *how to play golf;* to realize that a beautiful swing isn't enough; that strategy at times can be more effective than the swing.

In 1952 when I was seventeen, and a first-term summer student at Stanford, I won the United States Golf Association's Junior Girls' Championship at the Monterey Peninsula Country Club. Barbara McIntire, also seventeen, and National Amateur Champion of 1959, was runner up. Anne Quast (Decker), then fourteen, who started to play golf when she was three years old, and I were co-medalists with 76. Both Anne and Barbara are outstanding amateurs still. Anne, now married to a Tacoma dentist, has made her own golf history, winning the National Amateur crown in 1958 and 1961.

My winning the National Juniors and the resultant acclaim got me all fired up about golf. Psychology student or not, I was determined to make golf my career.

I started to wear glasses in 1953. I am nearsighted. At first they were hard to get used to on the golf course but they never bother me now. When it rains they can be slightly distracting for I have to stop to wipe them before every shot. (That also gives me a little time to think.) I don't like to wear a hat when I play, but I do wear a visor when it rains. I feel more secure with glasses on than without them; perhaps it's the knowledge that if I need to, with my nearsightedness, I can actually see what I have taught myself to feel in my golf swing. I tried contact lenses for a time but quickly discarded them. In the photographs illustrating my swing, I didn't wear glasses because photographer Robert Riger was fearful the sun would reflect in them and spoil a good picture.

My banner year as an amateur was 1954. I talked my father into letting me take a year off from school and financing me for a winter season on the women's tour in Florida and the Southeast. I headed cross-country in my own secondhand car, an asset as essential to a touring golfer as the golf equipment itself. I average 25,000 miles a year now on my speedometer, but I've never objected to it. It's all part of the game.

In the 1954 St. Petersburg Open, I lead the field of amateurs and pros with an opening day round of 68; the first time I ever broke 70. This brief taste of glory was a little too rich for my swing, and I scored 78–82 in the final two rounds, but I still finished low amateur for the tournament. I made a good showing in other tournaments which indicated to me I could play well enough to compete with the pros, so I returned to San Diego in March of 1954 and again persuaded my father to finance me for a few of the big tournaments that summer.

Figure 32   Harry Pressler, who helped make me a "square shooter," checks up on me.

In the Amateur Division, I won the Tam O'Shanter All American and the World Championship in Chicago; was runner-up to Barbara Romack in the National Amateur; low amateur in the National Open, finishing fourth among the field with rounds of 74–79–79–76. I played the final round with the late great Babe Didrikson Zaharias who, with a total of 291, won the Open that year for the third time (1948, 1950, 1954), fifteen months after her first cancer operation.

I turned professional that fall. My first year as a professional on the tour, 1955, marked the most frustrating phase of my golfing career, ego-wise, not economically. I won $6325.18 in prize money and finished twelfth among the lady pros for the year, but I didn't win a tournament.

I thought I had a good golf swing and people told me I had. I thought I hit the ball well, yet I'd go out and not score so well as I felt I should. I probably had as poor emotional control as any of the girls on the tour right now who aren't winning tournaments. I started tampering with my swing which is the most costly error a golfer can make during competition. No matter how you swing, in a tournament you've got to believe your swing is the right and only one for you, otherwise your confidence is destroyed and that's fatal to a golfer.

From 1955 to 1958 I went through a completely experimental period with my swing. I took lessons from Les Bolstad, a fine teacher at the University of Minnesota who works wonders with women; from Stan Kertes at the Bryn Mawr Country Club in Chicago (he was the Babe's first teacher in Los Angeles in 1933); from Harvey Penick at the Austin Country Club in Austin, Texas.

Each year I improved money-wise, but I still wasn't satisfied. Money has never been my goal in golf. Winning is.

In 1956, my second year on the tour, I won my first tournament, the Jacksonville Open, and $8253.66 for the year. In 1957, I won three tournaments, $11,131; scored a 75.38 average and was voted the Most Improved Player on the tour.

Still, I wasn't satisfied. I felt sorry for myself. I wanted to be better. I was wallowing in self-pity in 1958 after the St. Petersburg Open. I had finished out of the money and Betsy Rawls, my best friend on the tour, won the tournament. That only exaggerated in my mind my bad playing.

There is nothing more desolate than feeling sorry for yourself away from home, in a strange motel room with no one around to offer consolation or excuses for you.

"If you quit feeling sorry for yourself," said Betsy, a Phi Beta Kappa in physics and the most logical, levelheaded person I know, "you'd do better. You hit every golf shot yourself during this tournament. No one else hit

Figure 33

any of them for you so accept the responsibility for every shot you hit."

That was the most valuable golfing advice ever given to me.

I went on to win five tournaments that year including the U. S. Open and the LPGA, the first time anyone had won them both the same year. There wasn't a single shot I didn't say to myself, "This is your own responsibility. Do as well as you can, but make no excuses for yourself."

I know of no better Golden Rule for a golfer.

That year, I went to Harvey Penick who has been Betsy Rawls' teacher since she was seventeen and a student at the University of Texas in Austin. Betsy's own record in golf, the only four-time winner of the U. S. Open (1951, 1953, 1957, 1960) and winner of ten LPGA tournaments in 1957 is fantastic because unlike most champions she didn't take up golf until she was seventeen. It helps to get an early start in golf if you want to earn a living at it.

For two weeks, I took lessons from Harvey. At the time I thought he was the most frustrating teacher I ever went to for he never once mentioned anything wrong with my swing although I had gone to him because I thought I was hitting the ball badly. Maybe I expected him to be a miracle worker, but he didn't suggest one single change in my swing. A passive, patient professional, he quietly singled out good points in my swing and told me to concentrate on them solely as a means of getting the ball around the golf course.

That went in one ear and out the other. I left Harvey feeling hostile and cheated as if I had gotten absolutely nothing from those two weeks for which he didn't charge me, but I felt I had invested my time and energy. It took nearly two years before it finally dawned on me what Harvey Penick was trying to tell me.

The most important thing is to get the ball into the hole to the best of your ability.

It used to bother me terribly that I could hit two beautiful shots to a green and two putt for a regulation par, whereas my playing partner could drive to the left rough, send her second shot to the right rough and skull an iron onto the green ten feet from the pin, then sink it for her par.

Demoralizing? Yes. But not any more. Now, no matter how I get there, I'm happy to be there. I try to get there in the most nearly perfect way, but if I don't, I don't chastise myself, nor lose any time or concentration in self-recrimination.

My golf swing is no different now from what it was five years ago; however, since 1958, I've played many, many rounds of golf with Earl Stewart, Jr., the thirty-nine-year-old professional at the Oak Cliff Country Club in Dallas, Texas. In September 1961, Earl won the Dallas Open on his home course, the only club pro ever to win a PGA tournament under those circumstances. He shot a 67–72–68–75 to beat Doug Sanders, Gay Brewer, Jr., and Arnold Palmer, all who tied for second, one stroke behind.

Earl taught me how to play a round of golf so that every shot means something. All I demand of myself now is that the ball stays in play. I want something to swing at for the next shot. I don't want to be out of bounds or in an unplayable lie or in an impossible bunker or some ghastly spot in the rough or in the woods or behind a rock or under a tree.

Figure 34 Earl Stewart, Jr., and me. Earl is the Dallas Open Champion, 1961, and the only pro ever to win a PGA tournament on his home course, Oak Cliff Country Club, Dallas, Texas. We are being feted for our wins at a testimonial dinner in Dallas.

I want to be able to swing at the next shot.

When I stand up to a shot now, I ask myself: Where is the ideal place for me to hit this shot?

I look for it and at it. Then I look around it.

Then I ask myself: Where is the worst place I could hit this shot?

If my ideal spot is not too near the worst spot, allowing for the human element of margin for error, then I try to hit the ball to the ideal spot. But if trouble looms in the immediate area of the ideal spot, then I aim at the happy medium; an untroubled area where I still can swing for my par or whatever is the cheapest way, strokewise, out of the situation.

The best thing to do after a bad shot is not flail away again in anger and annoyance, but stop a moment, take a deep breath, then start swinging with conscious emphasis on maintaining balance and rhythm.

It's that "I'm going to get you out of here, ball, if it takes me all day" attitude that sends scores skyrocketing. Every golfer must get a definite mental positive picture of the shot to be played and then develop that picture through the muscles.

28   I'm always looking for the positive picture in golf, not the negative.

When I play my best golf, I feel as if I'm in a fog. Every good golfer feels this in different ways. Some feel "zeroed" in. They're not part of this world. They're standing back watching the earth in orbit with a golf club in their hands.

I think all winning golfers get themselves in a state of self-hypnosis while they play through positive concentration. The morning of a tournament I get a shaky feeling inside, perhaps "keyed up" is the better word. The days I play well are when I'm keyed up, at the right level, not too much or too little.

Figure 35　Chipping out of trouble to pick up par in the Mickey Wright Invitational Pro-Am, September 29, 1961.
COURTESY SAN DIEGO UNION PHOTOS

I overheard an amateur once ask Louise Suggs, "How long do you have to play before you get over this nervousness?"

"You never do," Louise admitted.

This is a healthy nervousness, for it alerts our muscles and our mind that every shot in golf is something unto itself and should be so considered.

The more I play, the more I respect the game of golf and its constant, never-ending challenge to me as a golfer and a person.

Figure 36 "Zeroed in" at Mission Valley Country Club, October 2, 1961.
COURTESY SAN DIEGO UNION PHOTOS

Chapter II

THE TROUBLE WITH WOMEN

ON THE golf course we women definitely are The Weaker Sex.

It's muscles, not mentality. From a standpoint of pure physical strength we cannot compete with men. The lady pros, pitted against the male pros, cannot overtake the 50-yard difference in a driver and the two-club length difference in an iron shot.

Someone once explained it to me this way. A human muscle is like a rope of fibers that contract. A woman's muscle is a comparatively little rope and a man's muscle is a bigger rope with stronger contractual power.

All humans have two kinds of muscles, the voluntary which execute movements prompted by the will and the involuntary which perform independently of the will. We recruit the voluntary muscles for the golf swing. They have to work when we tell them to and if we don't put them to work, they'll just be there doing nothing.

To compensate for this lack of strength, a woman golfer should have no wasted motion in her swing so she can utilize all those voluntary muscles to their maximum efficiency.

Good women golfers do. This is why I believe a woman can learn more from a good woman golfer. I believe, too, that if a woman understands more the whys and wherefores of the basic mechanics of a swing she can capitalize on that knowledge.

Apart from our comparative lack of strength, I think too many women golfers possess an even greater weakness on the golf course. *Women don't hit the ball as hard as they can.*

Too many women are so concerned they won't look graceful swinging hard at a ball that they end up with a most ungraceful powder puff caricature of a swing, looping, lunging, limp.

A psychiatrist and a golf addict, who liked to relate the two, cornered me once after a tournament to expound his theories, Freudian, of course.

"Do you know why women are afraid to take a divot?" he said to me so menacingly that if I were on a couch I would have slid down.

"Are they?" I said, completely intimidated.

"Are they!" he challenged. "I'll say they are! Women are afraid to take a divot because they don't want to damage the earth."

Figure 37

I'm no psychiatrist, but I am a golfer and a woman.

Dr. Freud isn't to blame, but the women are. Too many don't hit the ball hard enough to leave the imprint of their swing on the turf, let alone know when or why they should take a divot.

The late Mildred "Babe" Didrikson Zaharias was the strongest woman I ever knew. An Olympic star in javelin, hurdles, and high jump at the age of eighteen, she was also the greatest woman athlete of this or any century.

Golf was the Babe's greatest love and she succeeded in it despite the fact she didn't take it up until she was nineteen. Analytically, Babe's swing was not the best. She didn't transfer her weight properly to the right side, but she offset that by her magnificent power and co-ordination, her gentle touch around the greens, her putting prowess and her supreme confidence in her ability to perform. No shot was too tough for her to try. She was a great scrambler—and champion.

Babe hit the ball as hard as she could every time, with all that superb muscular power behind it. Not content with that, she practiced, practiced, practiced, especially on her short game and putting.

Even for her, there were no miracles in golf. She knew she couldn't wish herself into a good game. She worked at it and tried to understand how to get the most out of each shot.

The Babe was something unto herself as far as I was concerned. I could keep up with her and outhit her, but the Babe was the Babe with her glorious history of sports. Today, I am consistently the longest hitter among the women pros. I average around 225 yards a drive, a most satisfying average for a woman. I had a drive once in a Texan tournament that went ten yards over the green on a 385 yard hole, but everything was in my favor; a 40 mile wind behind me, the Texas hard pan to assist me, split-second timing, maximum power and clubhead squareness in the hitting area.

But, I frequently say to myself, if hitting the ball long were the only secret of good golf, why don't I win every tournament?

I don't. I win often, more often than most, but it is my swing, plus my savvy, plus my strategy, plus my short game that puts me in the winner's circle. I can outhit many men, much to their embarrassment, for suddenly they are pitting their masculinity against my femininity; their strength against mine. That's foolish. They aren't competing with my strength; they're competing with the efficiency of my swing.

Another Mickey, Mickey Mantle, and I have adopted Dallas, Texas, Big "D," as our home town when we're not swinging elsewhere for a living. Mickey and I have played golf together two or three times. He's a good example of why a good golf swing is important in hitting the ball.

When Mickey connects with a golf ball, he hits it a ton, but usually he

Figure 38 Why don't I win every tournament? Winning is a good feeling.

doesn't hit the ball much longer than I do because he doesn't contact the ball solidly. He tends to slice it. He moves the club to the outside; has his right elbow in the wrong position at the top of the swing and has the club-head coming outside in across the ball. He has a surprisingly good short game considering he doesn't have much time to work on it. He's a high 70 or low 80 shooter.

We have girls on the tour who win tournaments and don't average more than 200 yards on a drive but a 200-yard drive is a good average, especially if the ball is straight.

Mary Lena Faulk is typical of a fine lady golfer. She was women's amateur champion in 1953, turned professional in 1954, and won four LPGA tournaments in 1961, three of them in a row. Mary Lena hits the ball around 190–200 yards straight down the middle, is rarely in trouble and has a great short game. She chips well, pitches well, and putts well. I'd say she averages fewer putts per round than anybody on the tour.

I have never seen Mary Lena become outwardly annoyed with herself when she plays inadequately. I'm not advocating anger as a requisite of good golf, but I think if Mary Lena had more inner fire, more aggressiveness in her game, she would be an even better golfer.

A bad round of golf should provide the incentive to go out and work on

Figure 39 As I am after results, I use the club that will get me where I want
to go. COURTESY SAN DIEGO UNION PHOTOS

Figure 40 Giving instruction in the use of woods at a clinic.
COURTESY SAN DIEGO UNION PHOTOS

your game and improve it. I have noticed that many of our younger girls on the tour, after a particularly bad round, will come in and laugh about it. I don't think they should cry, but they'd be better off if they buckled down and worked at it so they'd have something to really smile about, a fine score.

Champions aren't made from the mold of indifference. Before my time on the tour, Patty Berg, who has done more for women's golf than anyone I know of, was playing a tournament in Tampa. She was leading, but on the final day she shot in the 80s and right out of the big win. Patty doesn't have those freckles and that red hair for nothing. She was so mad at herself she walked all the way home from the golf course to her hotel downtown, a distance of about eight miles.

Like me, Patty seeks the ultimate in golf. We have to. We're professionals. There is always someone younger, eager, able who wants to win and can.

I don't ask that you expect of yourself what I do of myself in golf. I can only tell you what I do. I win because I work at my golf and I am never satisfied with finishing second.

Women worry too much about the wrong things in golf. Some of their golfing values are false. When I swing a club, I am not consciously aware of my hands or my hips or my head or how I look swinging, factors which give other women undue—and hampering—concern.

For instance, a woman doesn't have to swing a heavy club to get better results. Most women, especially beginners, should use lighter clubs with whippy shafts which have greater flexibility and are designed as a substitute for strength to facilitate feel of the clubhead and allow for more clubhead speed at the hit. I use a lightweight men's club, a D-O Swingweight S-shaft, but I am a pro.

Women should rely upon their woods more, without fear of being criticized. We're after results and whatever club will put us where we want to be is the club to use.

A wood doesn't have to be swung as fast to loft a ball. A long iron, a two or three, commands great expertness in the hit. There is the same loft on a five wood as there is on a two iron, but if a five wood is easier to hit, then hit it.

It's how we get there, not what we use to get there, that's important.

I've given hundreds of clinics for women and told them what I feel are the basic mechanics of the swing and demonstrated the swing itself. As always, when I wind up a clinic, I recommend to the gallery to consult their club pro, whenever possible. After one clinic, a woman came up to me and said, very pleased with herself, "Mickey, I do exactly what you say, only instead of going to one pro, I go to two."

"Why two?" I asked.

"I go to one pro for my woods and the other pro for my irons," the golfing enthusiast explained, as if to say, "Doesn't everybody?"

She didn't realize it, but she was making the game of golf twice as difficult for herself by not accepting the idea that a swing is a swing is a swing and that she should swing the same way with every club; that only the club itself and the positioning of the ball change.

This is absolute truth. The entire game of golf is built upon this principle.

Chapter III

HAVE A BALL

Direction, Trajectory, Distance, The Grip,
Bottom Point of Swing

WHAT can happen to a golf ball?

A ball can go a certain direction, a certain trajectory or height, a certain distance, and that's all.

How can we control these three aspects of hitting the ball?

Ideally, we want to hit the ball straight. Two things only must take place to hit the ball straight. The club must travel from straight behind the ball and straight through at impact, and at impact, the clubface must be square to or perpendicular to the intended line of flight.

A club is "square" when the bottom line of the clubface is square to or perpendicular to the intended line of flight at a 90-degree angle on the ground.

How can we deviate from this perfection of direction?

If the bottom line of the clubface is at any angle other than 90 degrees to the intended line of flight at impact, the ball will travel either to the right or left of the target.

If the club travels from *outside in* across the line of flight, depending upon the clubhead position at contact, this outside-in direction of the clubhead will cause the ball to either fly straight left of the target, which is a "pull," or this outside-in direction will put a clockwise spin on the ball, causing it to slice to the right of your target. A sliced ball starts out straight at the hit, but at the end of its flight, the left to right spin on the ball takes over and the ball veers sharply to the right.

So, from an outside-in direction, you can go left or right of your target depending upon where and how the clubface contacts the ball.

If the club travels from *inside to the outside* across the line of flight, depending again upon the clubhead position at contact, the ball will fly straight right of the target, which is a "push," or this inside-out direction will put a counterclockwise spin on the ball, causing it to hook to the left

Figure 41   The Vardon overlapping grip.

of your target. A hooked ball starts out straight at the hit, but at the end of its flight, the right to left spin on the ball takes over and the ball tails off to the left.

With this explanation of what can happen when the club travels from other than straight behind the ball and straight through, I cannot emphasize strongly enough to you how important it is to have a good mental picture in your mind, before you initiate the golf swing, of that clubhead traveling straight behind the ball at the take-away, straight to it and straight through it at the hit.

This is a must as far as I'm concerned, and I personally draw this mental picture every time I hit a ball.

We are primarily concerned with the positive and not the negative aspects of this game so what we want to know is just what can we do to make this club approach the ball in the desired straight from behind straight through, clubhead square position.

Your hands are the only things that come in contact with the golf club so we will see that it is through their work by having a good or correct grip on the club at the address and throughout the swing that we will be able to return the club to the desired square position at contact.

The whole purpose of the grip is to position your hands upon the club in such a way that they will return to their original natural position at con-

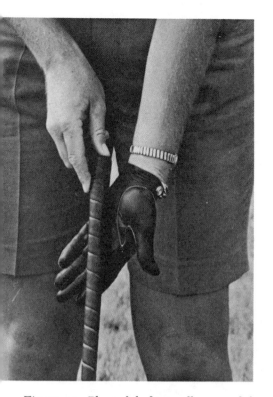

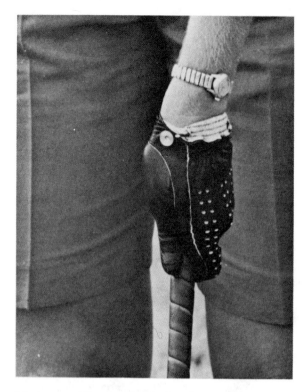

Figure 42　Place club diagonally across left hand.

Figure 43　The left hand closed upon the club.

tact. Throughout any swing, no matter how you grip the club, the hands tend to return to their normal position at the hit. Normal position of the hands is how they fall naturally when you stand up straight and let your arms dangle to the sides of your body. The palm of the left hand rests on the outside of the left thigh, and the palm of the right hand rests on the outside of the right thigh. The back of your left hand faces your target. The palm of the right hand faces your target.

This is how the hands should be on a golf club.

The grip that seems to best serve this purpose is the Vardon or overlapping grip (Figure 41), called overlapping because the little finger of the right hand hooks around the big knuckle of the index finger of the left hand.

After squaring the clubhead, grip the club with the left hand first. Too many golfers grip their club with the clubhead itself in a negative open or closed position.

Place the club diagonally across the left hand at the base of the fingers (Figure 42) so that when you close your hand around the gripping leather of the club, you have a combination palm and finger grip.

In looking at the closed left hand upon the club (Figure 43), you will see that the line formed between the thumb and index finger should be pointed in the general direction between the chin and the right shoulder.

39

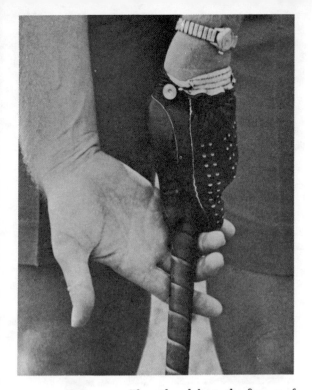

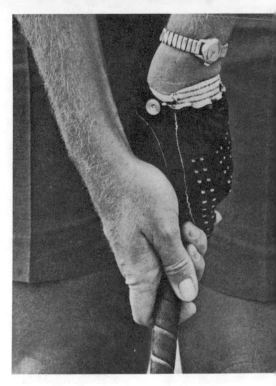

Figure 44 Place the club on the fingers of the right hand.

Figure 45 Close right hand, hold club entirely in fingers.

You should be able to see at least two and no more than three knuckles of the left hand. The left thumb will be slightly to the right side of the shaft. You should feel some inside gripping pressure in the line formed. Please notice I don't refer to the relationship of the thumb and index finger as "the V formed." I say line. To me, a V indicates a space between the thumb and index finger. I want *a solid closed line.*

This is a safety precaution to keep the grip from slipping which it is likely to do when there is a space for the club to slip into. This helps you particularly at the top of your swing because the club is firmly entrenched in your hands and gives you more feel of the clubhead itself.

In placing the right hand on the club, carry the club *entirely in the fingers* of the right hand (Figure 44).

In closing the right hand around the club, you will find that the left thumb should fit snugly into the natural diagonal hollow of the right palm, under the butt of the right thumb. Overlap the little finger of the right hand by hooking it around the large knuckle of the index finger of the left. I spread or trigger the index finger of my right hand so that there is a space between the index finger and *second finger* on the shaft. However, the line formed by the right thumb and right index finger is closed solidly, same as with the left hand. This line also should point in the same

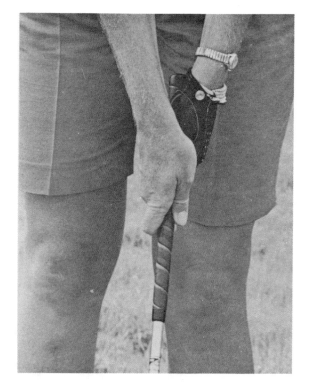

Figure 46   The slicer's grip—left-hand position.

Figure 47   The slicer's grip at address position.

direction as the line formed by the left thumb and index finger, toward the area between the chin and right shoulder (Figure 45).

This Vardon or overlapping grip brings the hands as close together as possible and allows them to hinge most efficiently in the swing. They are now in position to naturally return the clubhead to a square position at contact.

If a woman has trouble getting or maintaining the overlapping grip because her fingers aren't long enough to overlap, then I suggest she try the so-called baseball grip where *all the fingers* are on the club. The little finger of the right hand does not overlap, but otherwise this grip is exactly the same. The lines formed by the thumbs and index fingers should be positioned identically to the overlapping grip and there is no variance whatsoever.

To show you just how important the grip is, let's investigate what can happen with slightly different grips.

By positioning the hands upon the club so that the lines formed by the thumbs and index fingers point toward the *left* shoulder (Figure 46), you can see two to three knuckles of the *right* hand (Figure 47).

This is a so-called slicer's grip, but it is actually a pusher's grip. Holding the club in this position, swing it around you naturally, and you will find

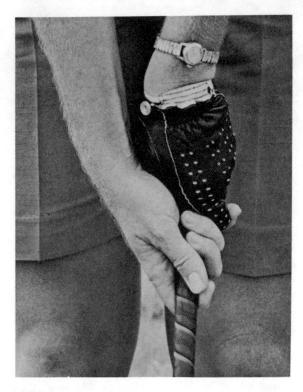

Figure 48   The hooker's grip—an unnatural
position.

that when the club returns to directly in front of you, your hands have
worked back to a more natural position with the lines pointing more to the
right shoulder than to the left as you deliberately positioned them. With
this grip the clubhead position at the ball is entirely different than with
the more natural Vardon grip. It is open, for the bottom line of the clubface
will be at right angles to a line considerably to the right of your target. This
would hit the ball straight right, which is a push not a slice, although the
ball has gone offline to the right.

We can also turn our hands in the opposite direction with the lines now
pointing *to the right of the right shoulder* (Figure 48). Now you can see
all four knuckles of the left hand. This is a so-called hooker's grip, again
incorrectly termed.

Holding the club in this position, swing it around you naturally, and you
will find this unnatural positioning of the hands has caused the clubface to
return to a closed or shut position, in which the bottom line of the club is
now at right angles to a line considerably to the left of your target, causing
you to hit the ball straight left, or pulled, not hooked.

Now it should be obvious to you not only what a good grip is, but how
essential it is to hitting the ball straight. Whenever the clubhead contacts
your ball other than from straight behind the line of flight, this has an im-

mediate effect on the direction the ball will travel. This direction is not only at the mercy of your grip, but your swing itself and in particular, your position at the top of the swing. I will break the swing down in detail later, but you should be aware of these key points in relation to direction.

A good right elbow position at the top of the swing will allow you to return the club on a correct line through the ball. A good right elbow position at the top of the swing is one in which the elbow points down toward the ground. *The line from the right armpit to the elbow will be parallel to the ground. This is only as high as you have to go to be at the top of the swing.*

From this right elbow position, you will find as you naturally return your weight from the right foot to the left, the right elbow is free to work down into your side in front of your right hip. This initial move from the top of the backswing is what insures the club returning on a good line through the ball, and you will notice in studying the pictures, I practice what I preach.

In contrast to this, if your right elbow is pointed out and away from the ground in a chicken wing formation, it becomes almost impossible to work the right elbow on the downswing in front of the right hip. This chicken wing formation is perfect lunge position and makes the clubhead immediately start working to the outside of your backswing plane and returns the club from outside in to your intended line of flight, causing the ball to either pull or slice in exactly opposite directions to where you want to go.

This outside-in position is the greatest trouble-maker in the swing.

Now we have discussed the direction in which the ball will go. Next point is the trajectory or height of the ball.

A ball goes *up* if you hit *down* on it. It isn't necessary to try to hit down on the ball to make it go up. The natural loft of the clubface and the proper positioning of the ball for the hit puts the ball into the air. If the ball is positioned and swung at properly, it will behave the way it should.

The position of the ball at the address determines whether or not and at what angle you hit down on it.

Every swing has a bottom point, that area of the arc where the clubhead contacts the ground or comes closest to it. The bottom point of any swing is determined by taking a practice swing. The bottom point of every swing changes according to the length of the club, the width of your stance, your position at address, the arc of the swing and the nature of the lie itself.

The closer you stand to a ball and the shorter the club, the more upright the swing will be. The farther you stand from a ball, the flatter the swing will be. The longer the length of the club the fuller the arc will be.

It is essential for you to know the bottom point of your swing with every club and position the ball behind this point but as close to it as possible with every club with the exception of the driver.

43

Figure 49   Positioning the ball.

To naturally hit down on a ball, all you have to do is position the ball an inch or two *to the right* of the bottom point of the swing. If you can contact the ball as near to the exact bottom of the swing as possible, the closer you will come to returning the clubhead to the ball with the exact loft upon that clubface with which the club was designed.

This isn't as complicated as it sounds.

For instance, with a number five iron, the bottom point of the swing will fall approximately midway in the stance. If we played the ball off the right foot with a five iron, we would contact the ball at a point in the swing when the full loft is not on the club. If we played the ball off the left foot with a number five iron—and were able to contact the ball in this far forward position—we would have added considerable loft to the club, for you have long since passed the bottom point of the swing and are hitting the ball with an ascending blow.

The driver is the one club we do not have to hit down on to get the ball up in the air because it is sitting on a tee. If we were to hit down on the ball with the driver, we would merely hit under the ball and sky it. With the driver, the ball is played off the left foot because that position is slightly

Figure 50   Relating the position of the ball and the stance.

ahead of or to the left of the bottom point of the swing and allows you to contact the ball with the club slightly ascending.

I am not giving here any exact specifics for the precise positioning within the stance for each ball to be played; the general area, yes, but not the precise point, for the bottom point of anyone's swing is dependent upon how he swings.

Generally speaking, with the short irons, the ball should be played some two to three inches to the right of the center of the stance. With the medium irons, four, five, six, the ball should be played at the center of the stance. With the long irons and fairway woods, the ball should be played some two to three inches to the right of the left foot. Play the driver directly off the left foot, heel or toe, whatever position fits the bottom point of your swing (Figures 49 and 50).

The difference between me and most other golfers is, I believe, the fact that I come closer to catching the ball at the exact bottom point of the swing than do other good golfers. This accounts for my hitting the ball relatively higher with each club than do the other topflight women professionals. This is because I have hit the ball with the original loft on the clubface, or as nearly square as it was in the address position, resting naturally on the ground, the way the clubhead was designed.

Most other good golfers catch the ball slightly behind the bottom point of the swing so they hit the ball more of a descending blow than I do.

As you can see, position in life is everything to a golf ball.

Now we know a ball can go a certain direction, trajectory or height and there is only one thing left; the distance a ball can travel.

In a standard set of golf clubs, the length of the shaft, the loft of the clubface and the weight of the club are so designed to pre-determine the different distances expected of each club.

The degree of efficiency with which these different clubs are swung will determine the distance of the ball.

Above all else, accuracy is the keynote of every club.

Each club is designed to do a special job. It is you who is the supreme executioner of each shot.

Chapter IV

A SWING IS A SWING IS A SWING

Balance, Rhythm, Address Position,
Lining Up Ball, Forward Press, Waggle

THERE are only three essentials *throughout my swing*.

1. Square clubface position
2. Good balance
3. Good rhythm

Why is a square clubface position the skeleton of my swing?

Because it is the only way I have found to most consistently have a repeating efficient swing. It requires no compensating moves or excess motion on the downswing. The golf swing is a reflective action. What you do on the way up, you must do on the way down. The simpler the swing, the better the chance of developing and maintaining it.

I want to be square not only at address and impact, but:

1. Halfway in the backswing (Figure 52)
2. At top of the swing (Figure 53)
3. Halfway through (Figure 54)
4. Finish (Figure 55)

At any one of these four points, if I were to stop the club and turn my feet and body so they faced my hands and clubhead, then placed the club upon the ground, I should be in relatively the same position as I was at address. The reason for this is I have maintained the relative position of my arms and elbows to each other throughout the swing. I am frank to say this takes time, trouble, and effort as it is an unnatural sustained positioning. The tendency when we swing is to let everything fly including our elbows. We want elbow control. You will notice in the above pictures I am wearing an artificial contrivance on my arms. It is an elasticized armband which I used in practicing to help strengthen and train the inside muscles of my arms for this elbow control. It is called a "Mickey Swing-Wright" armband and is manufactured and distributed by the Wilson Sporting Goods Company whom I have represented on the tournament trail since 1957.

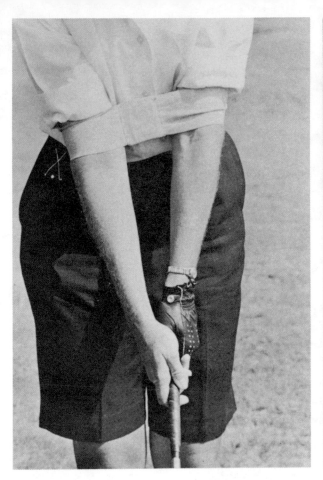

Figure 51 Correct grip for square clubface position at address.

Figure 52 Square clubface halfway in backswing.

Figure 54 Square clubface halfway through swing.

Figure 53   Square clubface at top of swing.

Figure 55   Square clubface at finish of swing.

I literally trained myself and my muscles to feel the clubhead in the pictured key, square positions. In golf I want to be a square shooter and to me a swing is a conscious feeling of the weight and position of the clubhead at all times throughout the swing.

If the first position, halfway back, is reached, more than half the battle of the swing has been won. From there, the momentum of the club should take you to the desired square position at the top of the swing. If that position is reached, the downswing again should take care of itself by the very nature of its own momentum, providing balance and rhythm are maintained throughout.

The only way I know to reach the halfway back position is through a one-piece move away from the ball in which my weight shift, via my feet and legs, my clubhead, hands, arms, shoulder turn, hip turn *all work together in a smooth, well-co-ordinated movement.*

How do I achieve that one-piece co-ordinated movement?

Through balance and rhythm.

Good balance in a golf swing is promoted by good footwork which not only gets the swing started but keeps it moving powerfully and efficiently back and through; from the left foot to the right foot on the backswing and returning it from the right, back to the left on the downswing.

I use a rolling across motion, as illustrated in the picture sequence that follows.

Figure 58 The recoil from this forward press sends weight back to and through address position, then across left foot toward inside of right foot in first move of backswing.

Figure 59 Weight moves *across* the left foot and over on to inside of right foot.

Figure 56 Address position of feet, legs and hands. Well-balanced, strong steady position. Weight from ball of feet back toward heels and evenly divided between both feet. Stance wide enough to maintain perfect balance throughout swing. I am *gripping-in* slightly on the inside of the right foot and inside of right knee. I'm using a seven iron.

Figure 57 Slight forward press. To start the swing, I make a slight forward motion with the right knee and move the weight slightly across the right foot.

Figure 60 Notice the left knee responds and moves in toward the right knee, a reflection of right knee action in forward press.

Figure 61 Club well into backswing—left heel beginning to lift slightly off ground.

Figure 62 Halfway point of the backswing. Notice, in figures 62, 63, and 64, the relatively slight change in the position of feet and legs. This indicates how quickly the weight transfers from left to right.

Figure 63 Near the top. I am well gripped-in on inside of right foot and with inside muscles of right leg. This allows me to transfer weight from left foot to right foot without swaying body, moving my head or losing balance.

Figure 66 Shows so very well how hand action in a golf swing is a responsive action to the transferring of weight. I make no conscious effort to move them. My right elbow at the top of the swing was pointed toward the ground and at the start of the downswing my elbow started its move to the inside of my right hip.

Figure 67 Pay particular attention to the thrusting or kicking off movement of right knee working with inside of right foot for return transfer of weight to the left. The fact that ball has been contacted first and divot taken afterward indicates ball was properly positioned for hit as ball was contacted before bottom point of swing and turf taken afterward.

Figure 64   Top of the backswing. Momentum of clubhead and turning of body have pulled left heel slightly off the ground. Knees remain close as in address position (figure 62) and right leg and knee slightly bent. This gripped-in and still flexed position is the strongest possible thrusting position to initiate a powerful downswing.

Figure 65   Beginning of the downswing. This is first almost imperceptible move of returning weight from right foot back toward left.

Figure 68   As the club swings upward in the follow through the right heel begins to leave the ground.

Figure 69   Weight is completely on left foot and right side is relaxed for completed finish.

Figure 70   At the completion of the swing the turn of body has pulled right foot off ground.

Because it is so difficult at first to learn to grip-in on the inside of the right foot and maintain this strong gripped-in position throughout the swing, this little exercise will help you train your muscles and strengthen this pivotal aspect of the swing.

Place a ball under the cleats of the outside part of right shoe (Figure 71). Then swing. To keep from falling off your right foot, you will have to make a conscious effort to grip-in with that right foot (Figure 72). This is a must in the swing so keep practicing it until you can feel the gripping-in of the right foot without the ball. This keeps you from swaying and overswinging. This also assists the feeling of kicking off or thrusting position for the transfer of weight to the left foot at the initiation of the down-swing; another must. While you practice, the ball under your shoe will act as a starting block.

Practice both these points until you can do it without the ball. Then never let the feeling go. It is pure gold.

This footwork, the mainspring of my swing, is aided and abetted by a strong address position, another requisite for a swing that will generate clubhead speed and keep you within the swinging plane you set yourself up in at address.

Too many people, I believe, feel so uncomfortable and off balance at address that it's almost impossible for them to get the swing started, let alone finish it.

The first step is seek your own level of balance at address.

Figure 71   Place ball under outside part of right shoe.

Figure 72   Grip-in with right foot and swing.

55

Figure 73   Bend forward slightly and the club, resting on the ground, becomes the third leg of the "tripod."

Figure 74   The right shoulder should be dropped slightly lower than the left.

It's no trick to maintain balance standing up straight, but you can't swing a golf club from this upright position.

Then, with a golf club in your hands, lower your center of balance, as if you were going to sit down. Automatically, this puts the responsibility of body balance upon the feet, legs, and knees. The knees are bent or flexed to compensate for your moving back the center of body gravity. Feel the distribution of weight principally upon the balls and heels of your feet. Now bend forward slightly at the waist to free your forearms from your body (Figure 73). Your upper arms rest lightly against the sides of your body.

The clubhead is resting upon the ground, the third leg of a tripod, as it were, in relation to your body.

You should be balanced. To make sure, have someone stand behind you and give you a slight push. If you topple over, you aren't sufficiently balanced to address a ball. Keep bracing and balancing with degrees of width of stance, lowering of the center of body, flexing of knees, distribution of weight with the feet, until you can remain balanced, with the club extended in front of you upon the ground, despite the slight push from behind.

Once you find your own level of balance, place a ball upon the ground. Your hands should be directly even with the golf ball or perhaps slightly to the left of the ball. The left arm should be fully extended though not stiff. The right shoulder should be dropped slightly lower than the left so the right elbow has the freedom to bend. At address, I keep the upper part of my arms firmly pressed against the upper part of my body (Figure 74).

This gripping-in of the upper arms, along with the gripping-in of the inside of the right foot, leg, and knee, are my checkpoints for the swing. The gripping-in of the right foot, leg, and knee keep me from overswinging and swaying. The gripping-in with my elbows alerts me that I want to keep them in this relative position to my body throughout the swing. At address, I can see the insides of my elbows, and if I were to look at them at the take-away from the ball to the point where the club follows the ground on the backswing, I could still see the insides of my elbows. This is all part of the square take-away from the ball.

I cannot emphasize too strongly the need for your feeling this gripping-in and a constant awareness of the relationship between the elbows throughout the swing. This must be a conscious effort as it is an unnatural positioning, but it's a must for the efficient one-piece swing.

Our tendency is to let everything fly, elbows especially, in outspread formation. A flying elbow is a pox as far as I'm concerned.

Although the elbows maintain their relative position, the arms move free of the body during the swing. If you were to keep them rigid to your body, everything in the swing would dip. Nor could you take the clubhead away squarely from the ball unless the yoke formed by the hands and arms followed the body turn straight back from the intended line of flight.

Barrel-chested men and well-endowed women should pay especial attention to this for upper arm positioning at address is an added problem.

The sequence with a half-seven iron that follows was taken to illustrate the one-piece move away from the ball.

The first six pictures (Figures 75 through 80) show how in a one-piece move away from the ball, the weight shift, clubhead, hands, arms, shoulder turn, hip turn work together to allow the club to be taken back in a low wide arc. Notice the relationship of my arms and elbows throughout this take-away and swing itself.

In Figures 81, 82, and 83 I have made absolutely no effort to deliberately cock my hands. The momentum of the clubhead from the swinging one-piece move has taken care of this for me until the hands reach the cocked position you see in Figure 84.

Figure 75 A strong, gripped-in address position. Figure 76 Square take-away.

Figure 79 Everything moves together. Figure 80 No obvious effort.

Figure 77   Still square and low.

Figure 78   Squarer still.

Figure 81   Clubhead starts its ascent.

Figure 82   Halfway back and still square.

Figure 83   Head hasn't budged.

Figure 84   Clubhead momentum cocks hands.

Figure 87   Still square after impact.

Figure 88   My favorite "shake hands" square position.

Figure 85   Attack position of downswing.   Figure 86   Body uncoiled for the hit.

It might appear also from studying the sequence that the clubhead is opening. This is more of an optical illusion, for the turning of the body is keeping the clubface relatively square. If I were to stop in Figure 82 and place the club down upon the ground, it would sit squarely, not open.

In Figures 85 and 86 all I am doing is returning the weight back from the right foot across onto the left foot. The uncoiling of the hips, shoulders, and hands on the downswing is completely a following action. Because this is only a half-seven shot and I'm looking for accuracy, not distance, the right elbow has hardly left the body throughout the backswing.

Compare Figure 81 to 87. This is almost a reverse negative of the square position away from the ball and through the ball.

Compare Figure 88 to 82. Here is another good test point, for in Figure 82 I could shake hands, with my extended left hand, and in Figure 88 I could shake hands, with my extended right hand. Again this is almost a reverse negative of halfway on the backswing and halfway on the follow through.

So saying, here's another test for you to ascertain whether or not you are in good balance during the swing. In a practice swing, stop the club at the top, with a deliberate effort to feel most of your weight on the inside of your right foot, leg, and knee, and then try putting the swing back in motion by shifting the weight back to the left foot. If you are able

61

to contact the ball solidly after this stopping, you will have proved to yourself that you are in a balanced square position at the top of the swing.

You should also be able to hold your follow through position for a second or two without losing your balance. This is merely a practice checkpoint, to build up your ego and your golf swing.

No golf swing can be built without rhythm. Rhythm to me is like a child's playswing. Once it is swung back in motion it will reach its own stopping point at the top and start down again of its own accord and momentum. No conscious effort should ever be made to interrupt, accelerate or slow down the natural motion and momentum of a golf swing, for good rhythm therein is a slow and gradual buildup of both power and speed from the time the clubhead addresses the ball until it contacts it and completes the swing with the power of its own momentum.

Any time you deliberately interfere with the natural rhythm of your golf swing, you're asking for trouble. You cannot consciously improve upon your own native, instinctive, inate rhythm. Rhythm is an entity onto itself. Like death and taxes, don't question it; just accept it. *You must.*

This is true in every shot in golf. Once you start that clubhead swinging back, let it have its head. Don't forcibly expend its energy until it does so of its own accord.

Rhythm is not to be confused with tempo. Tempo in a golf swing can vary from very slow to very fast depending completely upon the individual's personality and temperament.

I have a very fast tempo in my own swing. This certainly does not mean that my tempo would be right for you. No two swings are going to be exactly alike because like fingerprints, no two people are exactly alike.

But tempo is only the key that turns on the ignition of the rhythm.

You can't start a car from a dead start and put it immediately up to 70 miles an hour. No matter how powerful your engine, you must have a gradual acceleration of speed. So it is in a golf swing.

To me, the *waggle*, which is a release of tension, sets up the tempo and pattern of the golf swing. It alerts the muscles to stand ready to take the club back; lets you feel the weight of the clubhead and keeps you from developing too much high octane energy or tension. A waggle again is completely up to the individual, but no matter how you waggle to relieve your tension, a waggle should bear some resemblance to your take-away from the ball.

As much as possible, never waste any motion connected with any shot. Let everything you do contribute directly toward hitting that shot as well as you possibly can.

So saying, I am a strong believer in the forward press, to me the corner-stone of good rhythm. If you do not have or use a forward press, I strongly recommend you develop one. It makes the swing easier.

The clubhead itself is the heaviest part of the golf club. It is easier to start any relatively heavy object swinging with a forward motion than it is from a standing-still position.

A forward press in the golf swing is a slight motion to the left, initiated either with the hands, the left hip or the right knee. I use the right knee.

The right knee serves my purpose best because it represents exactly the reflexive action I am constantly seeking in my golf swing. A slight forward press with my right knee transfers my weight slightly across the right foot toward the left. The recoiling action from this starts my correct footwork from the left foot across to the inside of the right foot which sets in motion my one-piece swing and is the foothold and stronghold of my weight tranference throughout the swing.

The game of golf becomes easier if, from the very beginning, we establish a definite pattern of executing each shot. Begin with lining up the ball. In all the years I've seen Louise Suggs play, I've never seen her vary her procedure of lining up the ball one iota. From the time she selects her club until she strikes the ball takes no more than 15 seconds.

The best way to line up a ball is stand behind the ball and draw an imaginary line from your target back through the ball.

Always grip your club the same way. Square it on the ground, then grip it, left hand first. Check the positioning of the hands on the club. Do the lines formed by the thumbs and index fingers point to the direction of the chin and right shoulder? After a time you won't have to look at your hands to see if your grip is right. You'll be able to feel if they are in control of the club.

Pick out a spot three or four inches in front of your ball on the intended line of flight because you want your clubhead to follow that line after the hit. Step up to the ball; feet together, place the clubhead down behind the ball, square to the intended line of flight.

Without moving the clubhead, take your stance, commensurate with the club you are using and loft and distance desired. Look down at your feet. Visualize that straight line back from and away from the ball and say to yourself, "My clubhead will travel along this line." Without altering the position of your feet or your clubhead or your grip, go ahead and waggle, then forward press and the golf shot is underway.

Square clubhead, balance, rhythm, that's my Wright way to play golf.

Chapter V

THE FIVE AND SEVEN IRONS

THE FIVE IRON, which I'm using here, was known as the "mashie" to the old-timers, but it is a middle-iron in every sense; it's the middle iron between the one and nine iron and is played in the middle of the stance. A well-hit five iron shot will have more backspin on it than any other club in the bag. Even the experts can't figure out why. It just does. It'll land and stop.

Figure 89   Address position with five iron; weight evenly distributed both feet with slight gripping-in feeling inside of right foot and right knee, hands even with ball, ball played slightly left of center of stance, feet shoulder width, just wide enough to maintain balance throughout swing.

Figure 90   First move away from ball; club started back low and square for first six to eight inches, all part of one-piece move, left shoulder slightly higher than right; left arm extended though not stiff or rigid, elbows relatively close together, again with gripped-in feeling.

For this reason, perhaps, a five iron is the favorite club of many golfers. There is a danger to having a favorite club. It is likely to become a mental crutch, one we lean upon so much that when we must use a club other than our favorite, we don't have the same confidence in ourselves or our swing. Then those mental demons go to work and undermine the swing even more by nagging, "Remember you don't hit this as well as you do such and such a club."

No golfer can afford such a luxury. I swing every iron the same and I swing my woods the same way I swing my irons. The thing to always remember about irons is that they are the part of the game wherein you're mostly concerned with the direction in which you hit the ball. The distance gets progressively shorter with each shorter iron, so the need for accuracy in direction and distance becomes proportionately higher. There is less margin for error with an iron and the golf swing should become better and better the shorter the club and the shot. Not different, mind you, but better, purer and purer. Don't let fear change your swing. A mental picture of the swing itself and the shot to be played are musts for strategic iron shots.

Figure 91 Co-ordinated move of weight shift, hands, arms, shoulder turn, hip turn (figures 91, 92, and 93). Together all swing clubhead.

Figure 92 Hands have made no effort either to lift clubhead, or cock; momentum of clubhead from the one-piece move will do this.

Figure 93   Weight slowly being transferred from left foot across and into inside of right foot.

Figure 94   Halfway back, good example of club-face in relatively square position, toe of club pointed skyward, elbows still close together, weight has completed shift to right foot.

Figure 97   First move of downswing, discernible returning of weight back toward left foot, left heel settling back on ground, right elbow starting its move toward body. Everything else the same.

Figure 98   Halfway down; weight has returned to address position, hips have returned to square position as at address but shoulders still about 45 degrees turned, hands still in same position as in figure 96. Obviously, there has been no uncocking of hands or throwing of clubhead from top of swing. *Nor should there be.*

Figure 95 Momentum of club now swinging arms and hands into completed fully cocked top of backswing position. With a five iron, the club shaft does not quite reach a horizontal to the ground position at top of swing, as it does with a driver. The swing is the same, only length of club and resulting arc are different.

Figure 96 Square clubhead position. Palm of right hand is under shaft, shoulders are at 90 degree turn and hips 45 degree turn, right elbow pointed toward ground, line from right armpit to elbow parallel to ground, an automatic checkpoint to determine whether you have reached top of swing.

Figure 99 Hands now are about ready to uncock as involuntary muscular reaction to momentum of clubhead so clubhead can be released through the ball. Weight well over on left foot with noticeable thrust from right foot.

Figure 100 Impact; elbows in relatively same position as at address. Study closely here that clubhead is going to strike ball slightly descending blow. This is because ball has been so positioned near middle of stance that clubhead strikes ball just before bottom of swing point, taking divot afterward.

Figure 101 Halfway through; eyes still fixed on spot where ball was, right arm fully extended in handshaking position, left elbow bent, right hand just starting to turn club over. Compare this picture with figure 94, position at halfway point in backswing. It's almost an exact negative.

Figure 102 Right side is fully released with weight now entirely on left foot, momentum of club has swung hands toward high finish position.

A SEVEN IRON is one of the easiest clubs to swing for it's a perfect, relaxed, less demanding version of the full swing with a driver. If you can swing a seven iron with ease and confidence then transfer that swing and confidence to your other clubs and you are well on your way to a good golf swing.

Most people try to make the swing too difficult. It just doesn't seem logical to them that because a ball will travel the greatest distance with the driver, that that same little old swing that sends a ball hit by a seven iron a considerably shorter distance will suffice for the drive.

These doubting Thomases not only don't trust their swings; they don't trust their golf clubs or the manufacturers of golf clubs. The club itself is designed to hit the ball a certain distance. The only thing we have to do is position ourselves properly for each shot and each club and then swing to the best of our ability.

But don't change your swing for every club.

Change your club for every shot. Golf is tough enough. Don't make it even tougher for yourself by trying to learn more than one swing.

Figure 103 High finish position. Although my head obscures it, I can guarantee my left elbow is pointed toward ground, a reflection of my right elbow at top of backswing.

Figure 104 Completed, relaxed follow through, balanced so strongly I could hold position as checkpoint for proper and full transfer of weight to left side.

Figure 105 Address position from behind with seven iron; strong, well-balanced address, weight from balls of feet back to heels, knees slightly bent or flexed, in gripping-in almost knockkneed position, arms hanging comfortably from shoulders, neither hyper-extended nor cramped.

Figure 106 First move away from the ball. Everything working together. Clubhead square.

Figure 107　One-piece, co-ordinated move away from ball continues, weight shift, clubhead, hands, arms, shoulders, hips all working together effortlessly.

Figure 108　Halfway back; toe of club pointed skyward in desired square position, hands directly over shoelaces, left arm extended handshake position, right elbow slightly bent.

Figure 111　First move of downswing; weight starting its return from inside right foot back to left, left heel co-operates instinctively by starting to settle back on ground. Right elbow, too, makes its instinctive move by automatically working its way toward inside of right hipbone.

Figure 112　Halfway down; hips have returned to original square position, hands still fully cocked without conscious effort, shoulders still 45 degrees turned, your insurance toward returning club from inside to straight to and through the ball.

Figure 109 Hips have completed their 45 degree turn and shoulders their 90 degree turn, momentum of clubhead now swinging itself to completed top of backswing. Note especially, contraction of right leg muscles which indicates the gripping-in of right foot and knee. This is a must to prevent swaying and overswinging.

Figure 110 Top of backswing; the club shaft has not reached a horizontal to ground position, nor will it. It doesn't need to. This indicates control to me because with any short iron you don't have to swing the maximum for distance. You can always use a longer club. Here, as always at top of swing, clubface is square, right elbow pointed to ground, right palm under shaft and greater percentage of weight on inside of right foot, leg, and knee.

Figure 113 Immediately after impact; the thrusting and kicking off motion of right foot, leg and knee has turned the hips well to the left, permitting hands and arms to easily pass through parallel line of flight. Eyes still fixed on spot where ball was.

Figure 114 Club momentum is unwinding (or reverse recoil) body on through to expenditure of swing; carrying hands to high controlled finish.

Figure 115 Observe left elbow pointed to ground, right arm fully extended, left palm under shaft and elbows relatively close together, a complete reverse of top of backswing as seen in figure 110.

Figure 116 Completed relaxed expended finish of golf swing, weight almost entirely on left foot braced by leg and knee, body facing target in balanced hold-control position.

Chapter VI

STROKE SAVERS

*The Chip, Pitch and Run, Pitch Shot, Lob Shot,
Cut Shot, Wedge, Sand Iron; Uphill,
Downhill and Sidehill Lies*

A woman's short game is her substitute for strength and distance. Distance is no problem of mine, yet I work constantly on my short game. It is the frosting on the cake; the compensator for an error along the fairway; the difference between a par and a birdie; a bogey and a par; or worse.

A good short game is the greatest stroke saver I know.

A good short game, I think, depends 90 per cent on whether *you* think you have a good short game and can get that ball into or close to the hole.

A good short game is *feel* and *confidence*.

The mechanics of the short game are elementary, yet too many women disavow them. In chipping, for instance, they'll make a costly mistake of always using the same favorite club, saying, "I feel secure with this club."

This is a luxury none of us can afford. I vary each club according to the shot itself. To me a chip shot is one within a five-yard range of an unobstacled approach to the green. All I am looking for in a chip shot is for that ball to carry on to the green so it can roll the rest of the way to the hole. I can control a ball better if it is rolling than when it is in the air. The putt is proof of this.

The degree of carry I need for a chip affects my choice of club. I use:

A four or five iron from one to two feet off the edge of the green.

A six iron from three to four feet.

A nine iron from five to seven feet.

An eight iron from eight to eleven feet.

A seven iron from twelve to fifteen feet.

Since golf to me is a constantly imaginative game, I am subject to change without warning depending upon the conditions surrounding the shot; pin placement, contour and speed of the green, weather, and my instinct.

You must experiment yourself to find out how each club reacts under your own special touch.

Figure 117 Address position. I'm using a five iron. Feet very close together, weight on left foot, ball played off right heel, hands gripped to the bottom of the leather, almost to the steel, and slightly ahead of the ball to remove loft from the club. I'm as close to that ball as I can get.

Figure 118 Slight forward press with hands only. I want to catch the ball first and strike it solidly.

THE CHIP SHOT

With every chip shot, I always try to relate myself to the clubhead completely. I set myself up in a position where it appears and feels as if the left side is doing most of the work, I want no body motion or transfer of weight. The spot to where the ball must carry is firmly entrenched in my mind.

The closer you can feel to the ball and the more you can relate yourself to the clubhead, the better your chipping will be.

PITCH AND RUN

Outside of a five-yard range up to 20 yards away from the green, I play an approach shot which to me is either a pitch and run, or a pitch or lob or cut shot.

The lower the flight of the ball, the more it will roll. The higher it goes and the more directly down it drops, the less it will roll. This should be your

74

Figure 119　From the recoil of forward press with hands, the hands and forearms alone swing the club back. I want no excess motion in the body. I don't think about keeping my wrists stiff or cocking the hands, but rely completely upon my mental picture of the shot and natural instinct to carry that ball to my target so it will roll the rest of the way.

Figure 120　The backswing is fairly short; club-face square to ball, rhythm is steady throughout, not jerky nor fast, but controlled and smooth.

igure 121　Impact. The ball is ing hit a descending blow with little loft on the club as pos-ble, due to positioning of myself d the ball.

Figure 122　The right palm al-ways faces the target and never goes off line. This is my direc-tion finder.

Figure 123　I don't have to fol-low through much because the whole shot is so set up for the ball to run. The club should finish low along the ground.

mental gauge in choosing any club for an approach shot, bearing in mind the hazards ahead and the placement of the pin.

If I feel I cannot pitch a ball to carry to the green and roll it near the hole, then I resort to the pitch and run shot where the ball carries short of the green and runs on to it and toward the hole. This shot is very little different from the chip except there is slightly more body motion and response. Again I prefer a club with the least amount of loft, just enough to carry to my target short of the green so it will run the rest of the way to the hole. I use this shot when the pin is so close to the edge that I couldn't carry onto the green and still stop the roll of the ball close enough to the pin. Again, I imagine the edge of the green is right in front of me, and I visualize exactly where I want that ball to carry.

Although address, stance, and ball position are identical to the chip shot, allow for a longer backswing for the pitch and run and more body response, straight back, straight through. An apron will cushion a shot more than the clipped tightness of a green so the ball has to have a little more on it to land off the green and perform the way you want it to.

The pitch and run shot is very handy if you have a bad lie with the ball sitting down in a little divot where you can't pitch it with a more lofted club and carry it. Get it running as soon as possible. I rarely use any club higher than a seven iron for the pitch and run.

Figure 124 Address position. The mechanics in this lofted pitch shot are the same as for the explosion shot in the sand trap. Open stance; left foot drawn back from the intended line of flight; stance just wide enough to maintain balance, about 10 to 12 inches; ball played off left heel; aim slightly to the left of the target for this is a slice position; weight slightly on left foot. Hands even with ball to leave full loft on the club.

Figure 125 Club is taken deliberately *outside* the intended line of flight on the backswing in a one-piece swing; weight shift, hands, arms, shoulders and hips turning in unison.

Of all the short irons, the wedge is the most valuable club in my bag. It is the only club for which there is no standard distance, and I use it anywhere from 15 feet back of the green to 100 yards out. The wedge, and occasionally the sand wedge too when I want maximum loft and bite for an approach shot, is my trouble-shooter. It carries me over a hazard, bush, water, or whatever's in my way. I use my wedge for a high pitch or lob shot or cut shot.

For this loft shot, wherein I want the ball to bite as quickly as possible with a minimum of roll, my whole setup is different.

Balance, rhythm, almost a slow motion but forthright rhythm, and a completed follow through are musts for the lob or high pitch or cut shot.

Figure 126 The swing is about three-quarters, a fairly long swing because I am concentrating so hard on maintaining a slow even rhythm. I want the swinging weight of the clubhead itself to hit the ball the desired distance without any interference from me whatsoever to force or hamper that clubhead ac-

tion. The natural tendency is to try to help it, to scoop it or spoon it. Again picture in your mind the underhand action of tossing a ball to a target.

Figure 127 After impact. The club is swung through the ball from outside in across the intended line of flight, the same path of re-

turn as on the backswing. I make a special effort to retain the full loft on the club.

Figure 128 The finish. Notice that the club has been allowed to swing to a completed finish with no attempt to slow down or restrict its natural momentum.

The above holds true for the sand shot. The power of positive thinking is the most important psychological aspect of the sandtrap shot. It's the only shot in golf where you don't have to hit the ball. In fact, you shouldn't, for if you contact the ball without its collar of sand, you're going to fly it high or wide but not very handsome.

Trust your club for it is especially designed with a wide flange on the bottom to not dig in but bounce off the sand, taking whatever is in front of it with it. That's why a sand wedge is often called a "bouncer." It'll bounce if you give it a chance to.

In the sand I am so deliberate with the steadiness of my rhythm that I feel as if I could balance a bucket of water on the end of my club and not spill a drop. Yet this deliberateness doesn't prevent my letting the club-head do its work of swinging back down and through. Too many people dig their sand wedge right into the sand and bury it there as if they were planting a flag.

Don't dig, bounce and finish the shot.

The distance you want that ball to travel determines how much sand you should take behind the ball, generally an inch or two. Again this is feel and experience, something only you can find out for yourself. Remember the sand is contacted at the very bottom of your swing. In this case, the ball is your divot and it will fly after the sand is dislodged.

If the sand if wet, I still feel I'm playing the same shot, but I aim a little farther behind the ball; don't take as much swing and concentrate on a constant steady tempo. I rarely chip out of a sand trap. Once in a great while I do if the situation is ideal, no bank and the ball perched atop the sand with plenty of green for the roll.

If the ball is buried in the sand, then play it more off the right foot, close the face of the club and hit the buried ball a sharply descending blow.

With every short shot, you must have a definite mental picture fixed firmly in your mind before you execute the shot. Accuracy is what you're after and the ball can't stop where you want it to if you don't know where you want it to stop.

UPHILL, DOWNHILL, SIDEHILL LIES

These aren't part of the short game but I've included them here because you certainly save strokes by a better understanding of the behavior of the ball in these circumstances.

In an uphill or downhill lie, the problem is a matter of ball position. The secret is you must contact the ball as nearly as possible at the exact bottom point of your swing. *This is the time to take a practice swing and mean it.* Observe from your practice swing where the bottom point falls. You want to keep the full loft on the clubface as you contact the ball and you also want to keep that clubhead square to your intended line of flight in any of these lies.

Going uphill, the bottom point of the swing falls farther to the left or closer to the left foot than it does on flat lies. Downhill the reverse is true. The bottom point will fall much closer to the right foot than it does on a normal lie.

Before I hit the ball, I picture myself making the club follow the contour of the ground away from the ball and through the ball, and that's all I think about as I swing the club on these lies.

Uphill, I follow the contour of the ground on the backswing (Figure 129).

Downhill, I follow the contour of the ground through the ball as far as I possibly can (Figure 130).

On a *sidehill* lie, with the ball above or below your feet, you have two prime considerations; maintaining balance throughout the swing and anticipating the hook or slice reaction of the ball, for these lies are natural hook or slice positions because it is difficult to maintain the square to and through the ball position.

Figure 129 I'm using a five iron here. Ball is played left of center and weight is on the left foot.

Figure 130 Ball is played to right of center, weight evenly distributed.

Figure 131 Ball positioned in center of stance; played left of center and weight is on the left foot.

Figure 132 Weight balanced back toward the heels. Sitting back position.

With a sidehill lie, I take one club more and grip down on it somewhat as if I were taking a three-quarter swing. This is all with an eye toward maintaining my balance.

You'll be a lot happier if you make up your mind ahead of time that you're not going to hit as good a shot as you would if the ball were in a perfectly flat position. Also predetermine what the ball is likely to do and allow for it in your direction. Anticipate trouble ahead within hooking or slicing range. If there's a big fat trap within landing distance or water or woods, play short or wide of same.

When the ball is above your feet, sidehill, the natural tendency is to hook, for balance-wise, you tend to fall back on your heels. This brings the club inside-out across the ball with a closed clubface or hook position. Aim more to the right of your target. Feel as if you are balancing more toward your toes to counteract the tendency to fall back on the heels. Everything about this three-quarter swing has to be more compact to withstand gravity and maintain balance.

Once I set myself up for this shot, the only thing I think about is to mentally picture and feel as if I am working the *heel of the clubhead* straight through the ball. This helps hold the clubface square longer (Figure 131).

In a sidehill shot with the ball below my feet, I have to guard against being unbalanced in a forward position with the weight too much toward my toes. To offset this, I feel as if I am sitting more over the ball with my rear as ballast (Figure 132).

A downswing from a forward position will move the club to the outside of the intended line and approach the ball in an open or slice position. Aim more to the left throughout this compact, three-quarter swing.

Concentrate more on these shots, settle for less to begin with and you'll end up much happier.

The greatest book ever written on how to save shots on a golf course is published annually by the United States Golf Association. *The Rules of Golf* is the title and it sells for 25¢. Many clothing and sporting goods companies give away complimentary copies. I'm not going to waste your time or mine detailing any of those rules here, but I am constantly shocked, amazed, flabbergasted, and incensed at the golfers who don't know or bother to observe the rules. There is no excuse for it. A rule book should be as much a part of your equipment as the golf clubs themselves. Read it, read it, read it, and carry one in your golf bag.

Get in the habit of counting your clubs before each round. In the Tampa Open in 1956, I stupidly carried an extra five wood in my bag for 13 holes. I had a 26 stroke penalty. That was nothing compared to Mrs. Jackie Pung's nightmare in the 1957 Women's Open at Winged Foot when the stroke of a pencil disqualified her from the tournament which she had won. Although she had added her score correctly, she wrote down a four on a hole when she actually had a five.

A swing is a swing is a swing and a rule is a rule is a rule.

Learn them!

Chapter VII

THE PSYCHOLOGY OF PUTTING

PUTTING is a psychology, not a system!

Most fine putters are fine putters subconsciously. To be mechanically perfect isn't enough. If you have the feel of what you're trying to do, then the good points of the putting stroke will take place.

Billy Casper, one of the great modern-day putters, is from my home town, San Diego. When I play golf with Billy, I study and watch his putting technique. Several years ago, he made a comment on my putting.

"You hit *up* on the ball, rather than *down* on it," he said.

It wasn't a compliment. Just the reverse. Billy feels the ball should be struck a descending blow with the putter.

I think he really means the ball should be contacted without any loft on the club so the top half of the putting blade contacts the ball first. Then you're going to catch the top half of the ball right at the center or a little above center which makes the ball roll more directly off the putter blade.

Horton Smith, one of the greatest putters of the last thirty-five years, advocates complete squareness to the intended line; ball, stance, hands, putter blade at address and through the ball.

Yet another great golfer, Bobby Locke, hooks the ball on the putting green. Marlene Bauer Hagge, one of the finest women putters, tends to cut the ball. She takes an exceptionally wide stance to eliminate body movement and to keep her steady over the ball; plays the ball in the center of her stance and takes the putter blade back with the left hand and hits it with the right hand.

I have experimented with every possible putting grip, stance, and technique. Most of them worked for a time, then because I'm human, I'd lose confidence in that particular style and switch to another.

In recent years, my putting has become increasingly good because I have become more adept in the psychology of putting. I don't talk myself out of as many putts as I used to.

I used to stand over a six foot putt and say, "If I miss this, it gives me a double bogey and that'll put me six over par for a 78 and that puts me out of the money," or, in the same fatal negative fashion, I'd say, "You've got to get this one. That will put you even. You've got two holes left to play.

So and so is in with a certain score, and if you par the last two holes and sink this putt, you've got a chance.".

This is complete malignancy of the mind in putting.

My over-all rule now for a putt, once I am set up mentally and physically, is to block out everything else except the relation of myself to that club-head.

The trick of putting is to feel that you are the clubhead.

This isn't as nutty as it sounds. It can be done. Forget about everything except making that clubhead do exactly what you feel it has to do to get that ball in to or close to the hole.

I try to anticipate my putt long before I reach the green. I plan it with my approach shot, for I know wherever I land upon that green will determine the length and type putt I have.

In planning my approach shot, I mentally divide the green into halves and quarters. The pin is in one half and specifically in one half of the half, or quarter.

If the pin is in the front left quarter, I want my ball to be as close to it as possible whether the ball is on or off the green. I would rather be two or three feet short of the green, when it's tricky, with a comparatively easy chip shot than in a more troublesome spot on the green itself. This leaves me, hopefully, the more accurate shot, be it a chip or putt. Whatever it is, it's shorter in a more controllable area.

Quartering a green beforehand helps to relieve pressure. If I am shooting at a 4½ inch circle from 100 yards out, let's say, I'm going to be pretty unhappy if I don't get close to that target. But, if I give myself a target the size of a quarter of the green with thousands of square inches to shoot at, I'm taking pressure off myself and allowing for a better shot. If I aim for a 20-foot radius of the pin and land the ball 23 feet away, I've made a very small mistake, but if I were aiming squarely for the cup, I've made a 23-foot mistake.

If I am familiar with the green, its contour and grain texture—and it behooves me to be—I also try to aim for the quarter of the green or the side of the pin that will give me a downgrain putt. A ball breaks less rolling downgrain than it does into the grain. When a ball goes with the grain, the green is faster and the putt doesn't have as much time or inclination to go off line. Against the grain, or into it, the ball necessarily rolls slower. The blades of grass act as brakes so the ball has more time and impulse to respond to whatever slackens its pace.

Learning how to read grain is basically a knowledge of agronomy, but that isn't the solution. I never met a greenskeeper yet who had time to play golf, let alone putt on the greens he so painstakingly nurtures.

Reading a green is primarily a matter of instinct, feel, and logic. Generally, if the grass is shiny, as you look from the ball to the hole, the green is fast. If it's dull or darker, it's slower.

Bermuda grass greens, indigenous to hot climates, are tough and resistant and usually slower. Bent grass flourishes in moist climates and grows the way the name implies, in any direction. They're usually faster and also unpredictable.

"Away from the mountains and toward the ocean" is another rule of thumb for trying to interpret the roll of a green. First you have to know where the mountains and ocean are. That's where a good caddy can come in handy when you're playing a strange golf course. He can help you read the greens. I find it very satisfactory to try to figure it out by myself. In golf, I don't want to lean on any more crutches, mental or physical, than I have to. I'd hate to think my game would fall apart because I didn't have a good caddy. If you're not golfingly self-reliant, in judging distances, selecting clubs, and reading greens, your golf scores must be as variable as the winds themselves.

Figure 133   A good caddy can help me, but I have to rely on myself.

Any hard and fast rule about reading a green is subject to change without notice; wind, rain, manicured greens, neglected greens, bumps, holes, divot scars, an unseen pebble, or break in the green.

Consider also the green that undulates uphill and down, or downhill and up. Your only gauge here is touch and feel. You must anticipate the degree of hit to cope with either circumstance.

On a downhill putt, don't leave yourself treacherously short. On an uphill putt, don't leave yourself treacherously long or past the hole.

In stroke play, which is all we play on the tournament trail, we have to sink all putts. We never are given any so we never approach any putt carelessly. Each putt is counted until it's in. Match play, which is more frequent with amateur competition, has fostered many bad putting habits with the short or "gimme" putt wherein your opponent might give you putts from three to 18 inches, saying nonchalantly, "That's good."

They're so good you take them for granted, but suddenly you have a so-called gimme putt and your opponent doesn't say, "That's good." This is gamesmanship at its greatest.

Something new has been added. You're worried. Not only that but you're aware that your opponent has a defiant expression, as if to say, "Try to sink that one."

The only cure for this is to know that you're able to sink all putts so when the pressure is on you, you don't get puttitis, a disease I just made up, but which I have suffered from.

If they give them to you, of course, grab them, but never at the cost of undermining your confidence in these short putts.

When I come up to a putt on the green, the first thing I take into consideration is whether or not I think I should expect myself to make it. This isn't as negative as it sounds. If it's over ten feet, I'm actually saying to myself, "Don't expect too much of yourself so you won't be disappointed." Then, if I do make it, I feel as if I've been given a bonus.

Ten feet or under, I'm always gunning for the cup. Outside of that range, I mentally increase the size of the cup. All I want to do is get down in the regulation two. I never want to give myself a chance to say, "You idiot, you're a terrible putter. This is going to be a terrible day of putting for you."

Like everybody else, I hate a three-putt green like poison, and, like everybody else, I'll three putt sometime. In the 1960 U. S. Open, when I was trying to win my third consecutive Open—I had already won it twice consecutively which no one else had done, but I wanted to make an even better record—I three-putted myself right out of business.

At the end of the first 36 holes, I was seven shots ahead of my closest competitor, Betsy Rawls, who was my playing partner for the final 36 holes to be played on one day. Betsy shot a 68 that morning, which was magnificent, and I shot a 75, which was acceptable, but not in comparison to her play which I was witness to. She putted extremely well which you have to do to score 68.

In 18 holes, I had lost seven strokes, but I still was in contention for the final test of 18 holes. We both wanted to win so much and had put so much pressure upon ourselves that we each shot miserable 40s for the first nine holes. Meanwhile the rest of the field was gaining on us.

The turning point was the tenth hole. Betsy snapped out of this vacuum of self-pressure. I didn't. We both missed the green and had similiar pitch shots to the hole. Betsy hit first, within two or three feet of the cup. I completely let down and had no control over my emotions, swing-wise.

"Poor you," I said to myself. "Betsy got to hit first. There she is three feet from the hole. If you had hit first, perhaps the situation would be reversed. Then she would miss this shot the way you're going to miss this shot."

I missed it all right. I shot an 82 that final round and deserved every horrible shot and three putt. I had six three-putt greens. Betsy won. She was able to block out negative thoughts and concentrate. I wasn't.

I'm confessing to this only because I hope it will help you the way it has helped me. If you play the putt one stroke at a time, just like any other shot, you will become a better golfer.

The psychology of a three putt is to accept it and not assume that you are going to three putt again or that you're a bad putter.

In 1961, I won 10 tournaments, including the U. S. Open and the Championship of the Ladies Professional Golf Association. In 1958, I was the first woman professional to ever win them both in one year. In 1959, I won the Open, but didn't win the LPGA, and in 1960 I won the LPGA but lost the Open to Betsy, the sad story of which I've just told you.

My affirmative attitude on the putting green was the clincher for those great wins, plus my swing, my golfing savvy, and my one-stroke-at-a-time philosophy.

Here are the mechanics of my putting stroke:

I line the putt up from behind, engraining in my subconscious not only the line upon which I want to stroke the ball, but just how much of a stroke I will need to propel that ball the required distance. Then I step up to the ball. As with any other shot, when I address my putt, I have a spot picked out two to three inches in front of the ball over which I want that clubhead to travel, squarely.

For putting, I use a reverse overlapping grip (Figures 134 and 135).

The reverse overlapping is one in which all the fingers of the *right* hand

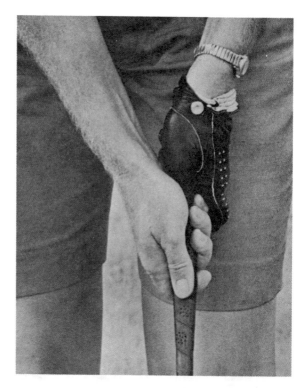

Figure 134 Place fingers of right hand on club first, then the left with index finger overlapping little finger of the right hand.

Figure 135 There is a definite sensation of pressure in the right thumb and index finger. I feel my control for distance and the hit with these two fingers.

are placed upon the club first, then the left hand is placed with the index finger of the left hand overlapping the little finger of the right hand.

I position my hands so the line formed by the thumb and index finger of the left hand is in opposition to the line formed by the thumb and index finger of the right hand. The line of the left hand should point in the direction of the left shoulder, and the line of the right hand should point in the direction of the right shoulder, as in Figure 135.

This positioning hinges the wrists in such a way so that for the squareness of putting purposes, the club can be kept more easily on a straight line back from, to, and through the ball. The only place I feel any definite pressure in the grip is in the right thumb and index finger. It is with these two fingers I feel my control for distance and the hit.

In the address position my feet are about 10 to 12 inches apart; weight balanced toward the heels (Figure 136). As much as possible, I want to relate myself to that clubhead. I move into a slight sitting-down position and comfortably bend forward from the waist in a combination of the two, enough to get my eyes directly over the ball. The ball is positioned off the instep of the left foot; hands even with the ball; right elbow resting comfortably on right hipbone; left elbow barely touching left side.

87

Figure 136 Putting—address position with weight balanced at the heels and feet about 10 to 12 inches apart.

Figure 137 Start putt with a slight forward press of the hands.

Figure 140 Hit ball with a slightly descending blow.

Figure 141 The follow through, like the back-swing, is abbreviated, with putter blade staying low to the ground.

Figure 138 Clubhead swings smoothly back away from the ball.

Figure 139 The backswing is relatively short and is controlled, as is the complete stroke, by the hands and wrists.

I start my putting stroke with a slight forward press of the hands. Again the purpose for the forward press is to start the clubhead smoothly swinging away from the ball. (Figure 137).

I use mainly a hands and wrists type stroke. I feel I can best control the ball this way (Figure 139).

I hit the ball with a slightly descending blow and the putter blade stays quite low to the ground through the ball (Figure 141).

These are the mechanics of *my* putting. To each his own in putting. Use whatever method gives you the most confidence and the best results.

I've said it before and I'll say it again. Putting is a psychology, not a system!

Chapter VIII

PRACTICE *CAN BE* FUN

No one can learn golf by osmosis.

The only way to strengthen your game and golfing muscles is to get out and practice.

To make practice fun, I play games. I don't want the drudgery of a long session on the practice tee, nor do I think it does any good. The minute I'm more concerned with having to do it than wanting to do it, I'm minimizing the benefits of practice.

If I'm tired, blistered, or resentful on the practice tee, I might as well go home. The practice will do me more harm than good.

By the same token, I have neither sympathy nor concern for those people who give lip service to practice by saying, "I'm wonderful on the practice tee, but I'm no good on the golf course."

Those people and others separate practice from the game of golf. The more closely you can relate practice to a playing round, the more you will benefit and lower your scores.

Every practice shot should mean something just as every stroke in golf must be counted.

When I go out to practice putting, instead of taking from three to ten balls on a putting clock, I take only one ball. "This is a round of golf," I say to myself. "I'm going to allow myself two putts per hole for the regulation 36 putts, but I want to see how much better I can do."

If on an 18-hole putting clock, I have a 33-putts total, I say, "Okay, if I made those three long putts on the course and didn't three putt any greens, I'd probably have such and such a score."

Then I try the 18 putting holes again to see if I can better it. This is the best way I know to practice putting.

If your practice putting green or clock—that's the terminology for a practice green—has only nine holes, then after you've played nine, reverse the procedure, so you're shooting in a different direction.

When I practice chipping, I take my entire set of clubs to the practice green. Instead of tumbling out a full bag of practice balls, I select six·balls and stagger them from a foot and a half off the green to 15 feet. I choose a target and start with the ball closest to the green. I execute each shot as I have outlined in the "Stroke Savers" chapter, and study the flight and action of each ball to familiarize myself with the performance of each club. Is it too short? Too long? Which club would have done it better? Did I position myself right? Did I feel the shot before I hit it?

I'm no mystic, but this pays off. After I've played the six balls, then I go up and putt each one to see how many of the six I can get down with in two from off the green. "Getting down in two from off the green" are to my mind the most beautiful words in golf.

To make things even tougher for myself, I set up a percentage of how many of those six I think I should sink in two. Personally, I settle for five out of six, but of necessity I set my standards high.

Three times, to simulate an 18-hole round, I play this game of "chipping six." I select a different target each time as a further challenge and practice payoff. At the most this game takes half an hour, and I have learned the equivalent of many 18-hole rounds of golf insofar as my chipping is concerned.

If you're fortunate enough to have a wide expanse surrounding your practice area, then all you do is move back with this game for the pitch and run, the pitch, the cut or lob shot.

Start *thinking* right now, practice-wise, with fewer balls hit and better, more constructive results.

I carry no more than from 30 to 50 balls in my practice bag. I shudder when I see people go to a practice tee with a bag bursting with 150 balls. Psychologically, it's the worst thing to do. Just looking at that pile of balls is enough to discourage you and encourage you to hit fast and furious without prejudgment and concentration.

Never, never, ever hit a practice ball without a target. If you do, you become sloppy, careless, and bad habit-forming. The pleasure you get isn't going to be worth the displeasure you get later on when it counts, on the golf course.

If your practice area, or driving range, doesn't have a target, create your own. Usually, I pick out a dark green spot or little bush or mound, within range of the club I'm using. Then just to make it tougher for myself, I encircle an imaginary green. "If I were to hit 30 balls with this five iron, how many of them would I expect to put upon the green?" I ask myself. Naturally, I'd like 30, but I'll settle for 20 or 25. That gives me something extra to swing at.

The practice tee lends itself to unlimited possibilities, much more so than the regular tee. Here is the perfect opportunity to practice everything I preach; consult chapter, verse, and pictures.

The square key positions; halfway in the backswing, at the top of the backswing, halfway through, at the finish.

Positioning of the arms and relative distance between the elbows throughout the swing.

For the fun of it, deliberately cut across your line of flight with the clubhead and see for yourself what happens to the ball when your clubhead approaches it from outside in and inside out.

Then compare that with the square position, straight away, to and through.

It's feel and awareness you're after and if you can find it on the practice tee, you'll have it on the regular tee.

Practice the transference of weight across the feet with the ball under the cleats of the right foot. You'll feel foolish and inadequate at first because it will seem so foreign to you. Don't discard the idea immediately in anger or impatience. It will pay off.

There should be a tranquillity of mind in practicing. It's time and energy expended for most valuable results. Always say to yourself, when you're at the height of exasperation, "If I were an expert I wouldn't be doing this, but I'm not an expert, and I won't be any good at all unless I try."

This is my anodyne for your future in golf. You will be better if you practice and *you won't be if you don't.*

In practicing, it's usually better to work with a short or medium iron because they're the easiest clubs to hit, due to the loft of the club and the shorter length. If you can get a good swing with a seven iron you should be able to use the same swing with every club.

If I'm working on something specific in my swing, I pick out a six or seven iron to start with because those are the clubs that are easiest for me to hit. I swing with either of these until the feel sets in, then I switch to the club that's been troubling me and swing exactly the same way, always, of course, letting the clubhead have its head and the length of its own arc and momentum.

If you're having trouble slicing or hooking the ball, this little practice will get you back on the road to moving the club from straight behind the ball to straight through quicker than anything I know.

Make two parallel lines of tees wide enough apart so that the clubhead can comfortably swing through (Figure 142). As you swing, try to picture the club returning from straight behind the ball and straight through without disturbing any of the tees (Figure 143). Naturally, if you knock over any of the tees, you've returned from a line other than straight behind the ball. In practicing, if you continue to knock the tees down, may I suggest you take two of your favorite golf clubs. Place them down parallel to each other, as a costly substitute for tees. Rather than nick your favorite club,

Figure 142   Place tees in two parallel rows.

this will put more pressure of concentration on you to make certain you bring the club from straight behind and straight through the ball.

Here's another practice "tee" gimmick. Place a tee from 10 to 12 inches directly behind the ball on the intended line of flight and see if you can knock that tee over each time with your square take-away, low along the ground, from the ball. This not only trains you and your muscles to keep the clubhead square in the take-away, but it will increase the length of your arc. Remember, the longer your arc, the more area the clubhead has to build up momentum.

Anybody who plays golf and is not satisfied with his game should have a golf club in his hands every day regardless of hitting balls. This is easily done; in the home, office, or backyard.

Keep an old or extra golf club around the house or office. A housewife doing her cleaning can keep a club in her utility closet. When she goes to get the vacuum cleaner or dustcloth, if she just picks up the golf club and practices the grip or swings that clubhead back and forth several times for the feel, she's helping her golf.

A heavy training club, weighing from 18 to 22 ounces, is a good thing to have around. Swing it, swing it, swing it. Get the feel.

Go out in the backyard and swing at dandelions or crab grass, but swing hard. Let go of your inhibitions when you swing. The old-fashioned method of beating a rug on the clothesline is what we're after. Hit it hard and purposefully.

Figure 143 Practice until you can hit the ball without hitting the rows of tees.

If you have a child interested in golf, keep a rubber mat in the back-yard or basement. Let them rid themselves of venom by swinging at that. But teach them how to grip the club so they can get the feel.

While you're in the kitchen waiting for coffee to percolate or water to boil, take your stance. Practice the gripped-in feeling of address. Transfer your weight from the left foot to the inside of the right foot, leg and knee. You don't always need a golf club in your hands to commit your muscles to move at your mental command.

While you're admiring or deprecating your figure in front of a mirror, try the one-piece move away from the ball, weight shift via the feet, hands, arms, shoulders, hips moving in a one-piece co-ordinated swing. Brace yourself against that right side. Don't sway or overswing.

I know I'm beginning to sound like a soothsayer. I don't mean to be. I believe all this. It can help. Besides it's good for you. It takes your mind off your other problems.

Practice does make more nearly perfect. Especially in golf.

On the tour, before a tournament the contestants usually arrive in the city two or three days ahead of time for practice rounds.

I prefer to play a practice round by myself early in the morning so I can experiment with terrain and distances. I look for trouble spots, strategic angles for approaches to the green, and test the contours of the greens. I'll deliberately hit shots into traps, both for psychological and sand soundings.

I'm literally feeling my way in a practice round. I don't want to prove anything other than to my subconscious storage of facts. If there are holes that demand shots I haven't used recently, then when I go to the practice tee, I'll concentrate on them.

This holds true particularly for women who rarely play outside their own golf course. It is their responsibility to know what shots they need most often and then concentrate upon improving them.

If the course is short, work on the irons. If it's long, work on the woods. If there's a par three that has you licked, take one club someday out to the practice tee, and don't do anything but hit to that imaginary green.

After all there are only 18 holes on any golf course and we're only permitted to carry 14 clubs in our golf bag. We should become familiar with each, the idiosyncrasies of every hole on our home course and the way every golf club we own reacts.

The morning of a tournament, I hit no more than 30 balls for my warm-up session. All I'm doing is loosening up my muscles and getting the feel of the golf club in my hands. I always start out with a pitching wedge and hit three or four balls without any thought whatsoever of the swing. Once I get the feel, then I skip every other club through the bag, hitting usually, the seven, five, three, and four iron; the driver and a fairway wood.

I try not to look for anything. I want the entire warm-up session to be nothing more than that. If I feel I'm not swinging well—and we all have days when we feel like that—I try to look at each shot to see whether or not the ball would have been in play on the golf course, or if it's a short iron, on the green.

I try never to walk away from the warm-up tee discouraged. I consider it a warm-up session only and am not looking for any flaws or trying to work a miracle in 20 minutes. This makes me swing easier and with more confidence.

"This is a practice tee," I say to myself, "and has absolutely no relationship to the caliber of fine golf I'm going to play today."

When I get on the course I concentrate on this:

1. Maintaining a relatively square clubface position throughout each swing.
2. Good balance throughout.
3. Good rhythm throughout.
4. One shot at a time.

This, to me, is the Wright way to play golf.

THE FINISH

A FINISH in a golf swing is a completed relaxed expenditure of the momentum of the clubhead generated during the swing itself.

This book is completed and I am relaxed for I have told in words and shown in pictures how I swing and why.

I think and do everything just the way I have said.

It has helped me.

I hope it helps others.

MICKEY WRIGHT

Figure 144